CHILD LABOUR IN INDIA
Rights, Welfare and Protection

CHILD LABOUR IN INDIA

Rights, Welfare and Protection

DR. DIPAK DAS
B.Com., PGDPM, LL.M., Ph.D. (Law)
Reader in Law
University of Burdwan
West Bengal

Foreword by

PROFESSOR AMIT SEN
LL.M., Ph.D. (London)
Ex-Dean, Faculty of Law, C.U.
Ex. Member
WEST BENGAL HUMAN RIGHTS COMMISSION

DEEP & DEEP PUBLICATIONS PVT. LTD.
F-159, Rajouri Garden, New Delhi - 110 027

CHILD LABOUR IN INDIA
Rights, Welfare and Protection

ISBN 978-81-8450-309-8

Typeset by RAHUL COMPOSERS
358, Pocket-B, Phase-2, Sector-16B, Dwarka, New Delhi - 110 075

Printed in India at MAYUR ENTERPRISES
WZ Plot No. 3, Gujjar Market, Tihar Village, New Delhi - 110 018

Published by DEEP & DEEP PUBLICATIONS PVT. LTD.
F-159, Rajouri Garden, New Delhi - 110 027 • Phone : 25435369, 25440916
E-mail : ddpubs@gmail.com • ddpbooks@yahoo.co.in
Showroom :
2/13, Ansari Road, Daryaganj, New Delhi - 110 002 • Telefax : 23245122

In Memory of

my beloved mother

Late Smt. Sova Bai

Contents

Professor Amit Sen
LLM PhD (London)
Ex-Dean, Faculty of Law, C.U.
Ex. Member
WEST BENGAL HUMAN RIGHTS COMMISSION

Foreword

"Child shows the man as morning shows the day"
—Poet Milton

The progress of any society would come to a grinding halt if the children of that society are not given equal opportunities and protection, irrespective of the families they come from, to develop themselves. Millions of children have been deprived of their basic rights simply because they are poor and are compelled to take up unhealthy and hazards jobs to make the both ends meet. Many talented and innovative brains can not blossom fully since the society is unable to provide education, health care, employment, etc. to them. The children are the future of the Nation. The nation gets eminent statesmen, distinguished scholars and philosophers, brave soldiers and patriots who, in fact, would determine the progress of the nation. Hence, the crying need of the hour is to protect children from exploitation and provide with all the basic necessities and amenities of life for their all round development. In turn they will devote their acquired knowledge and wisdom to build a strong and mighty nation.

I must appreciate Dr. Dipak Das, Reader in Law, University of Burdwan to write a book on the problems of the children of India who suffer from inequalities and disparities.

It is a great pleasure for me to welcome this authoritative assessment by Dr. Das on the burning issue of the day. The child labour is a curse to any nation and India is no exception.

Dr. Das is firmly of the view, and here I wholeheartedly agree, that the country has an important role to play in the gradual and orderly development of the children by enacting relevant pieces of legislations on the lines of international conventions relating to rights, welfare and protection of child labour in India.

The author has mentioned and thoroughly discussed the international instruments on child labour and urged the government to implement the various provisions of enactments to effectively deal with the problems of child labour. He has also reminded the government of the day of their constitutional obligations about the protection and welfare of the children.

Dr. Das has rightly pointed out the provisions contained in the UN Convention on the Rights of the child which India has accepted. This convention affirmed that the children's rights require special protection and it aims, not only to provide such protection, but also to ensure continuous improvement in the situation of children all over the world, as well as their development and education in conditions of peace and tranquility. As a signatory, it is the bounden duty of the government of India to respect and honour the international obligations so says the author.

The author has in unequivocal terms claimed that the Supreme Court has done commendable service in this field.

Dr. Das asserted that the Supreme Court, in order to tackle the problem of child labour, issued direction under the child labour (Prohibition and Regulation) Act, 1986 and directed that the offending employer must be asked to pay compensation for every child employed in contravention of the provisions of the Act. He maintains that this is a welcome decision in the right direction and this might discourage all the employers to engage child labour.

The merits of the book are many. Dr. Das has handled the topic competently and with scholarship. After meticulously going through the book, two thoughts cross my mind. First, when unclear and jargon loaded language is considered to be the hallmark of scholarship, it is pleasing to note a scholarly work in clear, simple and effective style. Secondly, it is redeeming to point out that an effective teacher thought it fit to devote some of his time in scholarly writing.

I find the book thought provoking and contains useful information relating to the problem of child labour. This book will, I firmly believe, be accepted by the legal fraternity as well as the NGOs working in this field.

All in all the book is a valuable contribution to the legal literature.

PROFESSOR AMIT SEN

Preface

The protection and welfare of working children has become a subject of paramount consideration now-a-days and no civilized society can overlook it. Children are future of the nation. It is, therefore, a duty of the every citizen of the nation to protect children. A society which functions within the framework of welfare state as envisaged in new Indian polity aiming at ensuring a minimum desirable standard of living to each and every member is obliged to come forward to understand the needs and problems of child labour and to undertake various measures that should be helpful on the fullest development of children on whom the future of a nation depends.

Politically, socially and economically child is the need of future national growth. Recognizing this fact, the Government, during last five decades, has taken various executive as well as legislative steps as provided in the Indian Constitution to protect children. However, in law much is to be accomplished. As a result, the employers take benefit of many loopholes in the law and exploit children. No empirical and fullest analysis of the problem has been attempted as yet to explore the means to abolish this menace truly. The purpose of this work is to make an humble attempt in furtherance of abridging this gap to provide real justice children in India.

The existing legal framework for employment of children is full of lacuna and loopholes as it suffers from internal contradictions. The greatest drawback of the laws is in its inadequate coverage. More than three-fourth of the child workers are employed in agriculture and allied activities but there is no law to take care of them employed in this sector.

Legislation by itself cannot achieve the objective of eradication of child labour. In countries, where child labour is rampant, the solution is unlikely to lie simply creating new laws or even ensuring that labour inspectors implement the existing laws. The adoption and implemention of laws needs to be supplemented by the social and economic measures with adequate awareness in masses.

The extension and improvement of schools to attract and retain children in it has been brought out as an effective strategy to wean children away from the work force. Child labour and compulsory education cannot co-exist. Education although will not by itself eradicate child labour but it will certainly reduce and discourage it. School going children can not provide their full labour force whole day therefore, they will not be beneficial to the employers in their business and ultimately the process may reduce the child labour in India. Education, besides enhancing the capabilities and welfare of children also has a positive impact on health, mortality, fertility and family life.

The most effective step to abolish child labour would be to improve the economic conditions of the families from where the children are drawn into the work force. The provisions of assistance in the form of income generating assets under different rural development and poverty eradication programme needs to be provided to such families having working children. The improvement in the economic conditions of the family makes a significant difference in the attitude of parents for making them conscious and boosts towards their children to schools. Majority of the poor people are keen that their children should get better jobs opportunities and improve their earnings in the future.

Thus, besides legislative measures, there is an urgent need to give importance to the supportive measures for child labour such as the removal of poverty and unemployment, enforcing compulsory primary education, medical and health support, proper nutrition, recreation and cultural activities, family planning, apprenticeship and vocational training.

The present study is an honest and relevant attempt to the problems relating to the child labour which has been analysed in the light of West Bengal with the help of empirical survey to explore the real problems faced by child labour. Therefore, to assess the real position and status of children at work and to ameliorate their condition, the present study in the most humble way tries to highlight on some of the relevant questions, such as, what age group children are engaged as child labour? What are the reasons behind their engagement as child labour? Do they work against their will? Whether they go school? Do the administrative agencies of the government help him? What steps have been taken by the government to eradicate this social evil? How is geographical condition of the place where child resides, responsible for engaging him/her into labour system? What is the role of people's representative or political parties towards this social evil, etc.? These questions necessitated to classify the whole study into six chapters.

Chapter 1 deals with introduction. Chapter 2 presents a review of international efforts made for eradication of child labour. Chapter 3 highlights on Indian existing laws, rules, regulations, etc. dealing with child labour. Chapter 4 discusses judicial efforts towards abolition of the problem of child labour. Chapter 5 presents full analytical discussions on the child labour problem in West Bengal based on empirical survey. Chapter 6 concludes the work with suggestions and recommendations to eradicate the child labour system in India.

It is expected that this attempt of the author would be meaningful in formulating consensus on the issue to eradicate child labour so that the dreams of the founding fathers of the Indian Constitution comes true.

Burdwan DIPAK DAS

Acknowledgements

It is a matter of great pleasure to express my profound gratitude to Prof. (Dr.) Shiv Sahai Singh, the Senior Professor of law, the University of Burdwan, Burdwan (West Bengal) who has supervised this project and guided me in pursuing this study to its socio-legal end, despite his busy schedule. I take this opportunity to express my sincere indebtness to Prof. (Dr.) S.S. Singh for devoting his valuable time for going through the draft and suggesting a number of amendments in it.

I express my gratitude to Head of Law department, Prof. Manik Chakarborty and ex-head of department Prof. S.K. Sadhu. I express my respect to Dr. A.H. Mondal and Dr. M. Momin, Professor of law for their valuable suggestions during the completion of the work. I would also like to record my sincere thank to Golam Ambia, Gobinda Pal, Mr. Sambhunath Chatterjee, Mr. Nilardi Ghosh, Mr. Kalyan Chatterjee and Mr. Ram Prasad Chakarborty of law department for their co-operation in all respect in completion of the research work. I will be failing in my duty if I do not express my thanks to my students particularly Binay Kr. Nonia, Supratim Roy and Shukla Roy, all LL.B (Final) 2004 for their co-operation during empirical survey of the project.

Mr. Suman Mukherjee, secretary of Bardhaman Sadar Renaissance Society (B.S.R.S.) and his friends have also been helpful during collection of data, I owe gratefulness to them. I also express my thanks to Mr. Pradip Chattopadhyay, Reader of the department of History, the University of Burdwan for helping me in translating the questionnaire from English language to Bengali.

My humble acknowledgement is due to the authorities and staffs of the library of Indian Law Institute, New Delhi, the Indian Society of International Law, New Delhi, Ministry of Human Resource Development, Govt. of India, V.V. Giri Labour Institute, Noida, Library of Supreme Court, IIPA, National Liabrary of Kolkata and Central Library of Burdwan University for their help in this academic pursuit.

I will be failing in my duty if I do not express my gratefulness to parents especially my father Shri Janthir Das and mother Late Mrs. Sova Bai and elder brother Shri Sajan Das who provided a congenial atmosphere to complete this study at home. Without their consistent inspiration, encouragement and active help probably this study would not have been possible.

In completing this study many known and unknown persons have guided, helped and assisted me and their suggestions have benefited me in a number of ways. I am grateful to all of them.

Last but not the least, I acknowledge Mr. Joydip Ghosh, proprietor of Raksha Kali Printer, Burdwan for happily feeding the draft into computer and obtaining the print-outs neatly and meticulously.

Burdwan DIPAK DAS

Abbreviations

AIEP	—	Area Intensive Education Programme
AIR	—	All India Reporter
CBCS	—	Community Based Convergent Service
CCA	—	Convergent Community Action
CDD-WASTERN	—	Control of Diarrhoeal Diseases Water and Sanitation
Cr.LJ	—	Criminal Law Journal
CSSM/MMCH	—	Child Survival and Safe Motherhood/ Mother and Child Health
DWCRA	—	Development of Women and Children in Rural Areas
DPEP	—	District Primary Education Programme
EAS	—	Employment Assurance Scheme
EFA	—	Education for All
HRD	—	Human Rights Development
ICDS	—	Integrated Child Development Programme
IIPA	—	Indian Institute of Public Administration
ILI	—	Indian Law Institute
IPC	—	Indian Penal Code
IDDCP	—	Iodine Deficiency Disorder Control Programme
IAY	—	Indira Awas Yojana

JRY	—	Jawahar Rojgar Yojana
JOY Learn	—	Joyful Learning
NGO	—	Non-Government Organisation
NLM	—	National Literacy Mission
PMRY	—	Prime Minister's Rozgar Yogana
RCHP	—	Reproductive and Child Health Programme
SC	—	Scheduled Caste
SCC	—	Supreme Court Cases
ST	—	Scheduled Tribe
SAFETY NET	—	Safety Net Programme
SHP	—	School Health Projects
SWATCH	—	Water Sanitation Programme
TLC	—	Total Literacy Compaign
TOT	—	Training of Trainers
TRYSEM	—	Training for Rural Youth for Self-Employment
UBSP/SJRY	—	Urban Basic Services Programme/ Swarna Jayanti Rozgar Yojana
UDHR	—	Universal Declaration of Human Rights
UNCRC	—	United Nations Child Rights Convention
UNICEF	—	United Nations International Children's Emergency Fund
WB	—	West Bengal

1

Introduction

Children are the national assets for future development of a nation. If a child is not provided attention, training and guidance, it will really be a shortcoming of government, every nation must, therefore, devote full attention to ensure that children are properly given care and attention in congenial atmosphere where they will have proper training, education and guidance for their overall development as a good citizen in future.

Now-a-days much interest is being shown in respect of welfare of children both at national and international level. Children are required special protection due to their tender age, physique and mental facility. They are required special law for their protection from exploitation, fraud and certain liabilities to develop their personality in view of weak position. The significance of child welfare lies in the consideration that the personally of man is built up in the early childhood and the physical and mental health of human resource of the nation is determined largely by the manner in which it is shaped in formative years. It is not an exaggeration to say that children are the blooming flowers of the garden of society and so, it is out duty to protect them from damaging effects of excessive exposure to heat, cold and rain. It is an established view today, that the children are the hope of parents and future of nation and therefore, they must be given adequate opportunities and facilities for their full development. The growth and development of a child into a mature and happy person with attractive personality mainly depends upon the care and attention he gets from the parent and society. If a child does not get proper education, diet and other basic amenities in formative years, his very development into a self-sustaining being is blocked. So it becomes the duty of every state to protect children's right by legislative and other means.

In 21st century, Human Resource Development is being given top priority in development, planning and policy-making by the Government. To achieve this goal, Government should be of great concern towards child development for an overall development of human resource. Child development is multifaceted psychological, sociological, economic and legal.

The growth of capitalism in the world has left serious effects on traditional family system. This has led to rural-urban migration in search of work and the traditional composite household to a "nuclear" family of parents and children. There is sexual division of labour due to inability of capitalist to generate employment for the potential workforce. In view of this division, man is expected to be the family breadwinner and the woman becomes secondary workers engaged mainly in child rearing and domestic work needed to survival of the family. Jointly the man contributed earning gained from labour market and the women does domestic work, thus both produce and reproduce the present and future force. During this process, parent's sexual division of labour is reflected and found in their children. Boys tend to anticipate to be father/husband/workers in the labour market and girls to be mainly mother/wife/housewife. Both boys and girls tend to adjust their personal development and skills to match these expectations, so that the foundation are laid to reproduction of sexual roles from earliest infancy. In a short period of 36 months, children develop their abilities to think and speak, learn and reason and lay the foundation for their values and social behavior as adults. Therefore, one of the important tasks of parent is to socialize the child this during formative years ensuring the right of the child at the every start of life. It should be the duty of government that the time of early childhood be given the highest priority attention while making decisions, laws, policies and programmes for the country.

Recent development is physical and social sciences have unfolded many dimensions of the entire process of personality development. They have shed sufficient light on different aspects of needs and problems of children and also on consequences that flow from it if those are not properly tackled. Recognition of these developmental needs of children and various deleterious effects caused by their non-fulfilment, have made it imperative for a society which feels concerned about its future in order to make it bright and prosperous, to take positive and concrete measures as may be helpful in adequately and appropriately satisfying the important needs of children and thereby providing them sufficient opportunities for their development as healthy and responsible members of tomorrow. The recognition of various harmful effects of child labour on physical, mental and moral development of children is commitment of the state to safeguard its children from exploitation and to ensure a healthy and satisfying life for them.

Child labour is not a new phenomenon to our age. What is new however, its perception as a social problem the world over. There has been a distinct change in the recent past in the attitudes and values of the legitimizing groups of society *vis-à-vis* child labour due to some new developments. In the pre-industrial agriculture of India, Children worked as helpers and learners in hereditarily determined family occupations under the supervision of adult family members. The work place was an extension of the home and work was characterized by personal informal relationship. The social scenario has, however, changed radically with the advent of industrialization and Urbanization, under the impact of newly generated centripetal forces. The protection of children has therefore, become an issue of paramount social significance in India as well as abroad.

Another factor highlighting the evil aspect of child labour in the recent advances in various sciences having a bearing on the child. Today, scientific knowledge has changed and revolutionized our outlook on the care of child including his developmental imperatives. Diffusion on this knowledge has changed a new awareness in the major institutions of society as to the relationship with his objects and his work. Child labour of late, has evoked deep concern. However, we must make a distinction between **'child labour'** and **'exploitation of child labour'**. Both are a problem through a different orders. Child labour as distinguished from work experience has mostly negative attributes. It can now be asserted on scientific grounds that work, as a direct fulfilment of the child's natural abilities and creative potentialities, is always conductive to his health growth. But work when taken up as a means for the fulfilment of some other needs becomes enslaving in character and deleterious in its impact. Labour is work of the latter type irrespective of the degree of strain or exploitation evolved in it. Labour in the case of child is especially harmful because the energy that should have been expanded on the untiring of his latent powers is consumed for purpose of base survival.

Keeping this in mind, the researcher has undertaken this research work to analyse and explore the child labour problems. It is not possible to review the situation through out the country. India, a vast country is not possible to be surveyed, therefore West Bengal is made sample area to conduct the empirical survey to explore and analyse the problem.

The study is intended to critically examine the problems faced by child labour both in organized and unorganized sector, and the laws, policies, rules, Convention and recommendations relating to elimination of child labour. Though a number of initiatives have been taken up in the recent past to combat problems of child labour in India, yet there is general feeling that most of these efforts have failed to realize the desired goal. The researcher is intended to focus on the problems through various angles using empirical survey in West Bengal to project a view of the whole country to enable the agencies, and planners, academicians and teachers involved at the level of implementation to target their efforts on the child labour families. With this thrust of problems, the major objectives of the study are as follows:

(i) To assess the position and family background of children engaged in labour system,
(ii) to ascertain the reasons for being engaged as child labour,
(iii) to highlight the existing Constitutional provision, legislative measures committed for eradication of child labour,
(iv) to bring out the attitude and perception of judiciary towards abolition of child labour,
(v) to examine the role of various agencies, such as personal, organizational, social, economic factors and forces influencing the quantity and quality for child labour.
(vi) to point out policy implication of findings and tentative suggestion and recommendations for eradication of child labour.

The study was thus taken up with the thrust to examine and assess the actual position, status and reason for child labour in rural and urban areas including the laws, policies, rules, regulation, Conventions and recommendations made for the purpose of abolition of child labour. With these objectives the present study has tried to investigate various aspects on determinations affecting and influencing the child labour problems and its eradication in West Bengal as well as in India. While investing these aspects several research issues or queries have been emerged like:

(a) What group children are engaged as labour and where do they work? The query has been based on the family background and nature of child labour.
(b) Do they go to school after or within they work? Have they come in this field against their will or otherwise?
(c) How does climatic/geographical condition of the place affect the incidence of child labour and what needs to done to eradicate this social menace.
(d) Is there any special measure adopted by the Government/Non-Government organization to help child labour.
(e) Do the Government/semi-Governmental organisations are really working to change their plight?

(f) What loopholes and intricacies are available in the laws, policies and rules made by government for the purpose of eradication of child labour?

(g) What is the reaction/response of the owners of child labour to the problem of children? Are the general public satisfied with the result of various laws and policies made for purpose of abolition of child labour. Do the children get benefited particularly through various schemes launched by government to help the children?

(h) What is the role of Government and Non-Government organisation towards eradication of child labour system?

(i) How far illiteracy of parent aggravates the problem of child labour?

(j) Are there any deficiencies or inadequacies or lack that the laws regarding child labour suffer from? If there is any, then what curative/supportive measures could be undertaken in this regard?

The magnitude of the child labour is too serious for a any simple plan of rescue and rehabilitation. The research work is undertaken with a hypothesis that the problem requires long term plan for its eradication.

Now, it has to be analysed explored to eradicate this menace from the society. The objectives devices, system including man power are to be feasibly seen for its abolition. Thus, the author anticipates with all devices legal, informal for the solution of the problem through this work.

This study is basically an assimilation of empirical as well as theoretical studies. For empirical study a Conventional survey method has been used for data collection which includes survey of some selected areas of sample universe by means of interviewing the sample data.

The Sample Universe of this study is the State of West Bengal.

The sample data of this study is limited to :

1. Child labour of different establishment, organization, etc., both female and male.
2. Proprietor/owner of child labour,

3. Concerned Government/Non-Government officials engaged towards elimination of child labour,
4. Local people from different occupations and professions.
   - (i) Personal interview with the sample data, i.e. the children engaged in labour system, the owners/ employers, government officials and local people, and
   - (ii) Primary records and reports available with mainly the Ministry of Human Rights Development, Govt. of India, Ministry of Rural Development, National Sample Survey Organisation, V.V. Giri National Labour Institute, Noida and also other government departments of Government of West Bengal.

While interviewing, in most of the cases it is found that whether it is child labourer, employer, general public or government officials, they preferred, informal discussion rather then filling up any printed questionnaires or from of question.

In interviewing children engaged in labour system as well as their owners, it is noticed that, though they are quite receptive to the researcher, at the same time they are quite apathetic to open their mouth. Only after repeated attempt to speak to the child labourers with full friendly gestures, they cooperated with author. Obviously, in every case the interview method has deliberately been made simplified and absolutely informal to make child labour and employers free, comfortable and informative. In order to have wide-range applicability the interview has been conducted in relaxed sitting where queries emerged according to the responses received from respondents to keep the flow of respondent's voice alive and it is noticed that in such an atmosphere the respondents used to feel interested and involved in discussing different aspect of their personal life. Sometimes interview has been initiated with a few pre-set questions for maintaining a broad framework for the enquiry particularity while interviewing government officials and staffs.

The Sample Universe has got an enormous reservoir of Secondary data. Those are several published materials like books, Journals, Magazines, Articles, Research paper, etc.

available mainly in Indian Law Institute, New Delhi, Society of International Law, New Delhi, V.V. Giri National Labour Institute, Noida, Indian Council for Social Science Research, JNU, New Delhi, Indian Institute of public Administration New Delhi, Ministry of HRD, Ministry of Rural Development, Ministry of Law, Ministry of Labour, Govt. of India, Labour Ministry of West Bengal and National library Kolkata.

The whole project is divided into six chapters for the convenience of its logical ends. *Chapter 1* deals with introduction. *Chapter 2* highlights the protection of children under international Law. *Chapter 3* concentrates on labour legislations and protection of children in India. *Chapter 4* discusses about judicial efforts towards elimination of child labour. *Chapter 5* explores and analyses field survey to highlight the problems as well as law and practice in the state of West Bengal. *Chapter 6* concludes the project with suggestions and recommendations.

2

The Protection of Children Under International Law

An Analysis with Special Reference to Abolition of Child Labour

The significance and the importance of the child lies in the fact that the child is the universe. If there was no child, there would be no humanity and there cannot be human civilization without humanity. Therefore, human being owes to the child the best that it has to be given. If there is no proper growth of child today, the future of the nation will be in dark. It is thus an obligation of every generation to bring up children in a proper way. Today's children will be the leaders who will maintain the prestige of the nation. If a child goes wrong for want of proper attention, training and guidance, it will indeed be a curse on the society. Every society must, therefore, devote full attention to ensure that children are properly brought up in a proper atmosphere in order that they may be able to have their rightful place in society in future.

However, the reality lies in the fact child still has not been given proper attention and being exploited by the people who achieve their selfish ends. It is possible to speak about children's right and their protection from different angles i.e. from Constitutional law, civil law, criminal law and of course, family law. But without doubt, it is family law that plays the most significant part in the protection of the child's interest, since it is this which regulates the relationship within the family 'the natural environment for the growth and well-being of all his members and particularly children'. 'For full and harmonious development' of the child's personality he or she should grow up in a family environment, surrounded by parents care and protection—one of the essential conditions of normal child's development. Every child 'as far as possible, has the right to know and be cared for by his or her parents'. At the same time the right of the child to a proper family upbringing is, in reality, his or her most significant personal right. How can we speak for protection of this if it is not even mentioned in law?

To perceive a child more as a subject than as an object of family relationship inevitably implies increasing parent's responsibility for their children. The right to family upbringing and to parental care must be equally granted to mentally or physically disabled children. Parents are obliged to bring up their children, and take care to their physical development and education. Violation of this rule, for example, by evasion of their duty of upbringing, abuse of parental rights, cruel treatment and harmful influence should be considered as penal offences entailing responsibility under different branches of law.

Human Resources Development has been given top priority in development and policy making. Child development should be of great concern for an overall development of this resource. A child is not expected to achieve a full physical and mental growth unless proper environment, adequate opportunities and sufficient facilities are provided. Child development is multifaceted Psychological, Sociological, economic and legal.

Most brain development happens before a child reaches three years old. Long before many adults even realize what is happening, the brain cells of a new infant proliferate exponentially synapses crackle and the patterns of lifetime are established because these early years are a time of such great change in young life and of such long-lasting influence, which ensures the rights of the child at the every start of life. Choices made and actions taken on behalf of children during this critical period affect not only how a child develops but also how a country makes progress.

No reasonable plan for human development can wait idly for the 18 years of childhood to pass before taking measures to protect the rights of the child. Nor can it waste the most opportune period for intervening a child's life, the years from birth to age three. The time of early childhood should merit the highest priority when responsible governments are making decisions about laws, policies, programmers and money. Yet, tragically both for children and for nations, these are the years that receive the least priority. Attention to the youngest children is most needed in countries gripped by intractable poverty, violence and devastating epidemics. With the global economy blooming, the majority of children still live in poverty while the wórld embraces the hope of peace, profit driven conflicts and ethnic battle erupt, risking the lives of children.

Although the particulars of their lives might differ, millions of mothers and fathers around the world, in both industrialized and developing countries, share the same story finding and making time, investing energies, stretching resources to provide for their son and daughters. Their days are consumed in helping their children in healthy protecting, teaching, guiding, and encouraging their talents and channeling their curiosity, delighting in their enthusiasm and their accomplishments. They search for advice and counsel from informal support network and community agencies as they struggle from great odds.

Today children are required to work individually without being given the personal and paternalistic guidance that they used to get in earlier times while working in family undertakings within or outside the precincts of their houses. They perform different types of repetitive, monotonous, unpromising boring and hazardous jobs and are quite often maltreated and exploited. The net effect of participation of children in work today is generally negative and harmful to their proper physical, mental and moral development.

The conditions of work are so bad that the various functions performed by children today have converted their work into labour. The children work on nominal wages for long hours without any rest interval, educational or recreational facilities beyond their capacity and against their wishes. The protection and promotion of interests of working children has become a subject of paramount importance today and no civilized society can afford to overlook it.

The global perspective on child labour evolved during this century. While child labour was previously viewed mainly in terms of wage employment in the formal manufacturing sector, today it is viewed more broadly, from the perspective of human rights and development. As a result, initiatives to address the problems of child labour have also evolved from normative instruments to multipronged approaches. These approaches fit under several categories, including:

- Promotion and enhancement of education,
- Strengthening of national and international legislation and improved enforcement,
- Empowerment of the poor,
- Social mobilization and community sensitization against all forms of child labour,
- Advocacy for increased responsibility among employers and corporations.
- General advocacy and awareness generation.

2.1 INTERNATIONAL INSTRUMENTS ON CHILD LABOUR

International legislation and discussions on child labour have had very important role in influencing national policies and shaping global understanding of the issue. As estimated 96 per cent of the World's children today are in countries where there is a legal obligation to protect children's rights in some form. International efforts to regulate child participation in work during this century date back to the ILO's minimum Age (Industry) Convention of 1919 which was adopted at its International Labour Conference. This Convention, ratified by 72 countries, established 14 years as the minimum age for children in industrial employment. It was followed by series of similar Conventions specifying a minimum age and regulating conditions of work in specific economic sectors and activities. However, the two main international instruments on child labour so far, are the ILO's minimum age Convention *No. 138 of 1973 and the UN Convention on the rights of the child.*

2.1.1 ILO Convention No. 138

The 1973 ILO Convention No. 138 concerning Minimum Age for admission to employment is a general instruments covering child employment across all sectors. It supersedes all prior ILO instrument applicable to limited economic sectors. Although, it has been ratified only by 49 Countries so far, it has helped to create international awareness about child labour and has influenced the formulation of national policies that prohibit and regulate child employment.

The Convention requires ratifying Countries to declare a minimum age of employment which is at least the age required to complete compulsory schooling and not less than 15 years and prohibits any employment under this age in any economic sector. It also obligates ratifying countries to undertake and pursue national policies for the effective abolition of child labour, and to progressively increase the minimum age for admission to employment to levels consistent with the fullest physical and mental development of young persons. Exceptions in scope and coverage are allowed depending on the nature of the work and the adequate of economic and educational facilities in the country. The Convention is supplemented by ILO Recommendation No. 146 which calls for the minimum employment age to be progressively raised to 16 and in the case of hazardous employment to 18. It also recommends that high priority be given to meeting the needs of children in national development policies and projects and that measures are undertaken to ensure the best possible conditions for the physical and mental growth of children and youth.

2.1.2 UN-Convention on the Rights of the Child (CRC)

The UN Convention on the Rights of the child is the most comprehensive international instrument on child rights and thus pertinent to the issue of child labour. It views investment in the physical, moral, spiritual and social development of the child as an imperative of all societies. As the most widely ratified human rights treaty in the world, the CRC has the widest legal force existing instruments of child labour. It was adopted by UN General Assembly in November 1989 and entered into force in September 1990 and is based on the Universal Declaration of Human Rights and the International Convent on Human Rights.

The CRC views the child in terms of a gamut of economic, civil, social, political and cultural rights. It constitutes the legal framework for the promotion and protection of all these rights in an integrated manner. It calls for the child's personality to fully prepare him or her for an adult life. All children must be ensured survival, personal and social development and physical, psychological and moral integrity. Special protection measures must be taken for those in especially difficult circumstances. The CRC obliges any ratifying Country to undertake all appropriate measures to help parents and others to fulfil their respective obligations in children (defined as less than 18) under the Convention and to make fundamental changes in their national laws, institutions, plans, policies and practices to be in consonance with the CRC's Principles. A fundamental tenet of the CRC is that all actions, under all circumstances, must take into account the "best interest of the child". Among the many rights protected under the CRC are the child's right to survival, to participation in society, to develop to full potential, to the highest attainable of health care, to free compulsory primary education to rest and relaxation, and to protection from all forms of sexual exploitation, abuse and illicit trafficking. Article 32 of the CRC, declares the child's right to protection from economic exploitation and from performing any work that is likely to be hazardous or to interfere with the child's education or to be harmful to the child's health or physical, mental, spiritual, moral or social development. It also calls for a minimum age of employment and regulation of working conditions to protect the rights of the child with appropriate penalties and sanctions for enforcement and for the immediate elimination of hazardous and exploitative child labour.

The CRC has played an important role in highlighting the

human rights dimension of child labour and influencing government legislation, policies and Constitutions. As of September 2002, 14 Countries had incorporated the principles of the CRC into their Constitutions, 35 had passed news laws or changed existing ones, and 13 built the Convention into the curricula or courses in educating children about their rights. Teachers, lawyers, police and judiciary have also been trained on the principles of the CRC in many countries.

2.1.3 OLSO Conference on Child Labour

The OLSO conference on child labour, held in October 1997, was based on broadly accepted international instruments such as the CRC and the ILO minimum Age Convention. It urged Countries to progressively eliminate all forms of child labour for children of school going age with priority to be given to the immediate removal of children from the intolerable forms of child labour and to their physical and psychological rehabilitation.

The conference called for action on various fronts to combat the problem. At the national level, countries were urged to undertake social and economic policies directed at poverty alleviation of concerned families and communities. It was also stressed that they establish cross-sectoral and integrated institutional mechanisms within the country for eliminating child labour. They were urged to improve statistical information on child labour with special focus on the girl child to establish multi-sectoral rehabilitation programmes for children withdrawn from work, and to encourage social mobilization through initiatives by trade unions, employer's organization and the non-governmental organizations. The conference highlighted on the importance of education particularly basic education in combating child labour.

At the global level, the conference urged international community to take several stepes, including increased poverty orientation programmes, facilitating the ratification and implementation of relevant international instruments, providing assistance to countries activity involved in the elimination of child labour, examining existing development co-operation programmes for their impact on child labour, and helping to establish improved information systems for data on child labour. The conference also made special note of the high risk faced by girl children due to sexual exploitation and child trafficking besides prostitution and urged the international community to provide special attention to girl child workers.

2.1.4 Other Conventions with Bearing on Child Labour

These include:

(a) The International Convent on Economic, Social and Cultural rights (entry into force : January 1976, ratified by 133 Countries).
Through this covenant, countries have to protect their children form economic exploitation and employment which hurts moral health and normal development. The countries are to provide age limit below which paid labourers would be prohibited or punishable by law. Some of these provision also relate to compulsory free primary education.

(b) The International Convent on Civil and Political Rights (entry into force: March, 1976, ratified by 132 Countries).
This covenant deals with the prohibition of slavery, servitude, forced labour and protection of minors.

(c) Supplementary Convention on the Abolition of Slavery, the slave trade, and Institutions and Practices similar to Slavery (entry into force : April, 1957, ratified by 114 Countries).
The Convention refers to the debt bondage of children.

(d) Convention for the suppression of the Traffic of persons and of the Exploitations of Prostitution of others (entry into force: July, 1951, ratified by 70 Countries).

2.1.5 International Land Marks on Child Labour

The 1990 world summit for childrens and its resulting world declaration on survival, protection, and development of children signed by over 150 countries, was an important international event with bearing on child labour. The declaration called upon countries to "work for the special protection of the working child and for the abolition of illegal child labour". It also supported by a plan of action which required countries to work towards ending the employment of children under hazardous and exploitative condition, for protecting such children, and for providing opportunities for their healthy development.

The 1990 world conference on Education for All was significant for child labour. Its resulting declaration called specifically for an understanding of child labour laws and for increased flexibility in the education system to be adapted to different circumstances for children.

More recently, there have been several meetings and resolutions on hazardous and exploitative forms of child labour. The declaration of the 1995 conference of labour ministers of the Non-Aligned movement and other developing countries refers of child labour as a "moral outrage" and "an affront" to human dignity and a plan of action was developed to eliminate child labour The Stockholm Congress on commercial sexual exploitations of children held in August 1996 put child prostitution formally on the global agenda for the first time. A declaration and Agenda for Action was also adopted at this Congress. Similarly, the Non-Aligned Movement Conference in New Delhi in August 1996, called for priority to be given in eliminating child labour in hazardous employment. *The third SAARC Ministerial Conference* on children of South Asia in August 1996, called for priority to be given eliminating bonded child labour by 2000, with total elimination of child labour in the region by 2010. A major Conference on child labour, organized by the Norwegian government, ILO and UNICEF was held in Oslo in October 1996. Child labour was also included in the agenda of the 1998 *International Labour Conference*.

The ILO has proposed a new Convention to bar intolerable forms of child labour that constitute a real affront to the conscience of human kind and that no society worthy of any name can tolerate, irrespective of its level of economic development. This Convention would aim at strengthening the existing set of ILO standards and at prioritizing the elimination of child labour. It would prohibit work performed by children in slavery including forced and bonded labour, the exploitation of children for prostitution or other illegal sexual practices, the use of children for drug trafficking, and the production of pornography. The ban would also include work, which exposes children to especially grave health and safety hazardous or prevents them from attention school. A law and practice report has already has been produced in preparation for this new Convention.[1]

2.1.6 Concept of Human Rights

As man became civilized, the rights of man were called as human rights. The human rights can be taken as gift of civilization. The struggle to preserve, protect and promote basic human rights continues in every generation and in every society. New rights arise from the womb of the old.

Human rights in the 20th century name for what have been traditionally known was a natural rights, which every human being everywhere, at all times, ought to have, simply because of the fact that he is rational and moral. No man may be deprived of these rights without grave affront to justice. The human rights or natural rights are sometimes to which every human being everywhere is entitled by virtue of the simple fact of being human. In more exhilarating phrase, it can be termed as the rights of man.

The expression human rights presupposes a level at which biological entities are bestowed with the dignity of being called human. Human rights denotes the enabling qualities of human being likely to assist him in realization of his potential as human being. It is the right of human being to life, liberty and equality before law. Freedom from exploitation, ecological harm and nuclear disasters can also be covered under human rights. At present human rights can be categorized as basic human rights and modern human right. These two categories can be further understood as right to bread and right to freedom. Freedom is the liberal rather modern conception of right and bread comes under the basic needs of human. Without bread, freedom of speech, assembly, association, conscience, religion and other political freedom may be meaningless. Under modern human

1. International Labour Office 'Children and Work', Geneva, November, 1996.

rights, every human being in this world should be able to live as a free, individual with adequate opportunity to mould his own future and to live as comfortably as he can be free from all kinds of fear. Freedom and well-being are the needs of every individual and there should not be any unnecessary, restrictions imposed on them either by other individual or by organized government. Freedom of speech and expression, right to move freely, right to from association, right to carry out any profession, occupation, trade or business trade or business, right to well being imply to development which means right to work, right to education, right to protection of environment, right to medical facilities, right against exploitation and free access to natural resources, etc., can be put under the modern Human Rights.

There is a conflict between basic human rights and modern human rights. Shelter for millions of pavement and slum dwellers have been demolished to construct five star hotels so that the rich and privileged can enjoy human rights. At one place poverty and starvation for people to sell themselves, their wives and children and at another large amount of food is wasted at big social gatherings. More than half of rural people do not have access to potable water but the urban people bathe in clean and fresh swimming pools. If only a handful enjoy human rights and the majority is denied basic human needs, the very notion of humanity is dismissed and such society will be called as basically unjust society which gives birth to condemned social evils like child labour, bonded labour, forced labour, slavery, peonage, etc.

The root of the development of human rights can be traced into historical documents such as Magna Carta (1215), Bill of Rights (1689), and the American Declaration of Independence (1766), which was modeled after John Lock's concept of natural rights. Similarly, the French Revolution (1789) laid down the right of man, the Congress of Vienna (1815) demonstrated international concern for human rights. The congress dealt with religious freedom and civil and political rights.

In the beginning of twentieth century, some principles of human rights were formulated before the era of the United Nations. Such principles and aims were already incorporated in the Constitution of the International Labour Organisation (ILO) established in 1919. The organisation's objective and aim was to ameliorate the position of working human being generally around the world. In 1924 under the initiation of ILO "Save the Children Fund International Union" promulgated certain rights of the child popularly known as "Declaration of Geneva". There were five basic principles for child welfare and protection. The same year the League of Nations for the first time attempted to codify the fundamental conditions to which the children have right. It was later revised and amplified in 1948 under the "Universal Declaration of Human Rights" (UDHR). The other humanitarian goals were set out the convent of the League of Nations specially article 23[2] and article 25[3] respectively. In 1930 ILO adopted Convention No. 29 laying down that, "each member of the ILO which ratifies the Convention undertakes to eradicate the use of forced or compulsory labour in all its forms within the shortest possible period" (The Convention came into force on 1st May, 1932). The Convention also provided for necessary measures to safeguard the health of the workers and to guarantee the necessary medical care. This was the period in which international solidarity was based on collaboration and mutual assistance in all fields to promote human welfare that could not be achieved due to break of World War II in 1939.

Through out attempt was made by the covenant of league of nations and the ILO Convention of 1930 to give shape to human rights but the human rights did not become the concern of international politics or law after IInd world war. Earlier, how a state treated its own citizens was considered to be its own

2. "The covenant of the League of Nations, Article 23, states in part" subject and in accordance with the provisions and International conventions existing or hereafter to be agreed upon, the members of the league (a) will endeavour to secure and maintain fair and human conditions of labour for men, women and children both in their own countries and in all countries to which their commercial and industrial extend and for that purpose will establish and maintain the necessary International organization.
3. The convent of the League of nations, Article 25 states: "The members of the league agreed to encourage and promote the establishment and co-operation of duly authorized voluntary National Red Cross Organisation having as purpose, the improvement of health, the prevention of disease and the mitigations of suffering throughout the world".

business. There was no serious disposition to render the treatment of the individual human beings in his own country, a subject of international law and diplomacy. In 1944 (i.e. within the continuing phase of the II World War) another attempt was taken by the league of Nations and ILO "The Declaration of Philadelphia",[4] but it also turned to be a futile at time and later attained effectively through the ILO Constitution. The wave of revulsion arose from shocking crimes committed against humanity during the Second World War. The far reaching effects of the IInd world war could be assessed with its end on 14th August, 1945, which created a favour of human rights not only in the war devastated countries but more or less throughout the world. Human right made through a dominant position in U.N. charter and United Nation officially came into effect on 24th October 1945. The U.N charter came to be recognized as the first basic instrument laying the foundation of the law of the International Human Rights. Consequently ILO got a moral boost and become specialized agency of UN in 1946 and with unique co-operation both UNO and ILO went ahead with their Conventions, recommendations, declaration and International Covenants not only in their field of International Human Rights but also they accorded special protection of child and child labour in many cases through their Conventions, recommendations, declarations and International covenants because they set out "hard law" as binding instruments for states once ratified and on which effective promotion and defence of human rights could take place.

In this context let it be mentioned that the sole credit for creating the milestones of peace in the International sphere of Human Rights specially Rights of child does not go to UN or ILO only, but also to United Nations International Children's Emergency Fund (UNICEF), [UNICEF established in 1946, to meet the emergency needs of the children, particularly in the

4. Declaration of Philadelphia, 1944 recognises the solemn obligations of the ILO to further among the nations of the world programmers which will the effective recognition of the right of collective bargaining, the Co-operation of management and labour in the continuous improvement of productive effectively, and the collaboration of workers and employers in the preparation and applications of social and economic measures.

war devastated. Countries, UNICEF is not a special agency, but a subsidiary body of the General Assembly reporting to the Economic and social council] for its valuable contribution though Investigation, Reporting and Research to formulate effective covenants and standards for protection of children.

2.1.7. United Nations (UN) on Protection of Child

The first vital and bold move taken by UN after its formation in the international sphere was the *Universal Declaration of Human Rights*, which was adopted by the General Assembly of the UN on 10th December 1948. It makes specific, the general character of human rights including the rights of child. The declaration is a remarkable juncture of political, civil, economic and social rights with equality and freedom from discrimination. It sumps up the civil, political and religious liberties for which men have struggled so long. It also contains new economic and social rights and are being recognized today. The preamble to the Declaration stressed the "dignity and worth of the human person". The aims of this declaration are started categorically within 30 (thirty). Articles of Declaration. Basically this declaration aims at protecting the liberty, physical and moral integrity of human person including the right to life, freedom from slavery, servitude and forced labour freedom from torture, or from cruel, inhuman or degrading treatment or punishment, the right to freedom from arbitrary arrest or detention, the right to fair trial, the right to privacy, right to freedom of thought, conscience and religion. The universal declaration of Human Rights formulated by United Nations with care and deliberations, setout the common standard that should apply to Human Society, irrespective of race, colour, sex, language, birth or other status. In effect, it sets forth the attributes of a democratic system and with respect to the function of the rule of law. The declaration is a declaration and does not have much binding effect, therefore, this declaration has been converted into two covenants:

> *The Covenant on Civil and Political Rights 1966* came into force on 23rd March 1976 and contain a bundle of Civil and Political Rights),

The Covenant on Economic, Social and Cultural Rights 1966 (came into force on 3rd January 1976 and contain a bundle of Economic Social and Cultural Rights); and

An optional protocol to the Covenant on Civil and Political Rights 1966 providing machinery for complaints from individuals.

Apart from the Universal Declaration of Human Rights there are various subsequent U.N. instruments which seek to deal with the human rights specially. As for example protection of the human being in his very existence, the elimination of racial discrimination, the protection of women, the protection of children and child labour, the protection of workers, the protection of refugee and stateless persons, the protection of combatants, war victims, civil population, etc.

After the 2nd World War, on November 20th 1959, the United Nations General Assembly with representatives of 78 countries meeting in plenary session adopted ten point Declaration on the Rights of the Child unanimously. The spirit of the document was reflected in the preamble, which said in part "mankind owes to the child the best it has to give". The declaration contains the preamble and ten principles and being issued in consonance with philosophy contained in the United Nations Charter, Universal Declaration of Human Rights, 1948, the Geneva Declaration on the Rights of the Child, 1924; the statutes of specialized agencies and international organizations concerned with the welfare of children. Besides laying down the general obligation of the men and women, institution and governments towards the child the declaration, it specifically lays down that the child is not to be admitted to employment before an appropriate minimum age and is not caused or permitted to be engaged in any occupation or employment which would prejudice his health or education or interface with his physical, or mental development.

Next dominating step by UN was the *Convention on the Right of Child 1989*. This Convention was intended to purge the shortcomings of the previous declarations on the rights of the child and all the previous declarations were to supplement this declaration. The major reason for choosing 1989 is the symbolic importance of that year. It marks the tenth anniversary of the international year of the child. This declaration is setout in preamble and Articles the Convention declares that "children all round the world have equal rights, irrespective of their religion, ethnicity or sex". Article 32 being the most important Article of the Convention at first, states the definition of child labour. "Any work that impedes the social, physical and emotional well-being of the child is considered child labour (or child exploitation)". Next this article bids that State parties to recognize the rights of the child to be protected from economic exploitation and from performing any work that is likely to be hazardous or to interfere with the child's education, or be harmful to the child's health or physical, mental, spiritual, moral or social development". All member-states of the UN have ratified this Convention.

2.1.8. ILO (International Labour Organization) on Protection of Child

As far as action by the ILO itself is concerned, virtually all of its activities under its different programmes are aimed at making reality of the rights and freedoms proclaimed in the Constitution of the ILO, they also are effective means of implementing many of the rights mentioned in the *Universal Declaration of Human Rights* and the International Covenants of Human Rights which are concerns of ILO. ILO's work in the field of Human Rights aims interalia at safeguarding freedom of association; abolition of forced labour; elimination of discrimination in employment; promotion of equality of opportunity, protection of children from economic exploitation, minimum wages, social security and adequate conditions of work and life.

So far ILO has adopted 18 Conventions and 16 Recommendations in the area of employment of child labour. These relate to various phases of the employment, i.e. minimum wages for employment of children, medical examination of child labour, prohibition of night work for children, conditions of employment of children in underground work and their training, etc. Conventions are generally set out under the defined heads of scope, object, theme, exceptions, prior, consultation and enforcement, but Recommendations generally carry Observations and suggestive notes.

The various ILO Conventions and Recommendations relating to the employment of child labour are as under:

(a) Minimum Age

(i) Minimum Age (Industry) Conventions, 1919,
(ii) Minimum Age (Sea) Convention, 1929,
(iii) Minimum Age (Trimmers and Stokers) Convention, 1921,
(iv) Minimum Age (Agricultural) Convention, 1921,
(v) Minimum Age (Non-Industrial Employment) Convention, 1932,
(vi) Minimum Age (Sea) (Revized) Convention, 1936,
(vii) Minimum age (Industry) (Revized) Connection, 1936,
(viii) Minimum Age Non Industrial Employment) (Revized) Convention, 1937,
(ix) Minimum Age (Fisherman) (Revized) Convention, 1959,
(x) Minimum Age (Underground Work) (Revized) Convention, 1956,
(xi) Minimum Age (On Minimum Age) (Revized) Convention, 1973,
(xii) Minimum Age (Coal Mines) Recommendation, 1953,
(xiii) Minimum Age (Family) Recommendation, 1937,
(xiv) Minimum Age (Non Industrial Employment) Recommendation, 1932,
(xv) Minimum Age Recommendation, and 1932,
(xvi) Minimum Age (Underground Work) Recommendation, 1965.

(b) Medical Examination of Young Persons

(i) Medical Examination of young persons (Industry) Convention, 1946,
(ii) Medical Examination of young persons (Non Industrial Occupation) Convention, 1946,
(iii) Medical Examination of young persons (Sea) Convention, 1921, and

(iv) Medical Examination of young persons (underground Work) Convention, 1946.

(c) Night Work of Young Person

(i) Night work of persons (industry) Convention, 1919,
(ii) Night work of young persons (Industry) Convention, 1945,
(iii) Night work of children and young persons (Agriculture) Recommendation, 1921, and
(iv) Night work of young persons (Non-Industrial occupation) Recommendation, 1946.

(d) Miscellaneous (8 other Recommendations)

(i) *Apprenticeship Recommendation, 1939,*
(ii) Conditions of Employment of Young Persons (underground work) Recommendation, 1965,
(iii) Lead Poisoning (women and children) Recommendation, 1919,
(iv) Special Young Schemes Recommendation, 1970,
(v) Unemployment (Young person) Recommendation, 1935,
(vi) Vocational Training (Fisherman) Recommendation, 1966,
(vii) Vocational Training Recommendation, 1939, and
(viii) Vocational Training Recommendation, 1962.

It was only about a hundred and fifty years ago that the issue of child labour began to emerge as a matter of concern in Europe and in the U.S. This concern initially centered on the long hours and grim conditions under which children worked in sweat shops. No reader of 19th century of English literature can forget the graphic accounts of the condition in which children worked in factories and workshops or the horrors of little chimney sweeps climbing of soft filled chimney to clean them, so vividly described in the novel of Charlos Dickens and others.

It was however only in the 20th century that child labour began to be seen as a matter of global concern for all nations and peoples of the world. The forefront of the emerging concern against child labour was the International Labour Organization (ILO), set-up as a part of the treaty of Versailles after the first world war, whose guiding principle of social, justice militated against the child labour. Starting from the preamble to the construction of the ILO, the concern for protecting children from the effects of premature work was reflected in the many Conventions that the ILO adopted against the child labour. The first of these was the Convention No. 5 which prescribed a minimum age below which no person could work in industrial establishment. This Convention was adopted by the ILO in the very year of its inception in 1919. Convention No. 5 was followed by a serious of 11 Conventions that went on to lay down norms for the employment of children in many other sectors of employment like agriculture, railways, mining, sea-faring and plantation, etc.

By the 1970s world option against the child labour had developed to the stage where there was a strong need felt to set international standards against child labour in all sectors of employment. Thus emerged Convention No. 138, which was adopted by the International Labour Conference of the ILO in 1973. This Convention is a flexible instrument that fixes different minimum ages not only for different forms of employment but also for countries at different stages of economic development. Thus, in a country like India the minimum age for normal categories of work is 14 while for the same categories of normal work the minimum age in a developed country is 15. The minimum age for entry into an employment increases to 16 to 18 respectively for developing and developed economies, in the case of hazardous work and work that is likely to endanger the health, safety and morals of children. The minimum age falls to 12 to 13 respectively in the case of light work. The principal point about this Convention is that all forms of child labour are prohibited below the age of 12. The status ratification of Convention No. 139 by the international community has been very disappointing. Only 54 countries have ratified this instrument as on 1st July 1997. Neither India nor many developed countries including the US have ratified it so far.

Another significant recent international development on child labour is the unanimous adoption of the UN Convention on the Rights of the child, more popularly known by its acronym CRC, by the UN General Assembly in November 1989. The CRC seeks to protect a wide range of children's right including the right to protection from economic exploitation and from performing any work that is likely to be hazardous or to interface with their education or to harmful to their physical, mental, spiritual, moral and social development. The CRC requires states parties to take legislative, administrative, social and educational measures to ensure the implementation of the Convention and in particular to provide for :

Specifying minimum age or minimum ages for admission to employment.

Appropriate regulation of the hours of work and condition of employment.

Appropriate penalties or other sanctions to ensure the effective enforcement of its provision.

The CRC also contains important provision which have a bearing on extreme forms of child labour, such as the sexual exploitation of children and the abduction and sale of trafficking in children for any purpose or in any form. The CRC is one of the most ratified international instruments on any subject in the world. So far 189 countries of the world, all excepting the US and Somalia have ratified the Convention.

The last decade has witnessed an explosion in global interest in child labour that has manifested itself in various forms. One form has been the growing concern amongst western consumers that the products that they buy and use should not have been made by children. Consumer concern has manifested itself to boycott of goods produced by child labour and through encouraging purchase of only products that are labeled free to child labour. There has also been active concern amongest governments of many western countries that the growing numbers of child laboures world wide would childhood on the hand and the future economies of these countries on the other. Government interventions have been taken various forms but most significant amongst them has been the positive act of international efforts against child labour.

Thus the German offer of finding of the *International Labour Organization's Technical Co-operation Projection* child labour led in 1972 to establishment of the International programme on the elimination of child labour (IPEC). IPEC is today funded by about a dozen countries and has about 30 countries participating in it. Governments have also stepped up funding of child labour projects through bilateral conduits, many western governments today channel funds for child labour through their development agencies in Africa, Central and South America and Sough East Asia. A third measure of government's concern against child labour is the increased public attention on the subject, reflected in the growing debate on child labour within international agencies like the ILO, UNICEF, UNDP, etc. International conference on child labour like the recent OSLO conference are examples of government support in building up an international environment against the child labour through mobilizing world public opinion against it. While there has been growing talk in some countries of bringing in domestic legislation against the import of goods manufactured by children and of trade sanctions against countries that do not discourage child labour, no such laws have as yet been put on the statute books in any country or in international statute books.

The growing public opinion against child labour is reflected also in the initiatives being taken by NGOs in developed countries and significantly in those developing countries where child labour is endemic. We not only see a greater NGO involvement and action against child labour in Europe and the US , but a similar increase in NGO activity in a country like India during the last decade. International attention on child labour is likely to grow in coming years. This attention is both a challenge and an opportunity for a country like India, facing with the largest member of child labourers anywhere in the world. The future of India's children, its human capital formation and its economic growth would largely be decided on how the country copes with this challenge and exploits the opportunity that the present climate of international opinion on child labour provides.

2.1.9 The Role of ILO: Present and Future Perspective

The organizations Constitutional instruments have been drawn as a legal basis for certain important standards. This has been the case for two passages, how well known, in the declaration of Philadelphia of 1944, which has been incorporated into the ILO Constitution. One of these affirms that "all human beings, irrespective of race, creed or sex, have to right to pursue both their material well-being and their spiritual development in conditions of freedom and dignity of economic security and equal opportunity, the other, that freedom of expression and of association are essential to sustained progress". There are no empty phrases. They have provided the legal framework for concrete action on a large scale, both to safeguard trade union freedom and to combat racial discrimination. They have made possible an evaluation of the behaviour, the law and the practice of states, and they have permitted recommendations to be made, where necessary, for corrective action or even a change in Social Policy.

At the other end of the standard setting spectrum will be found standards which are less formal than conventions and recommendations, such as resolutions adopted by the Conference, some of which on trade union freedom and human rights, have often been seen as a basis for decision of the ILO supervising bodies, and for the case law of these bodies.

It is however principally the Conventions and recommendations—which have formed the foundations of ILO action for the protection and promotion of both economic and social rights (employment, conditions of work and life, social security, employment of women, children and special categories of workers, social institutions, etc.) and certain fundamental rights and freedoms such as freedom of association, the abolition of forced and the elimination of discrimination in employment.

At this stage, certain essential question must be clarified.

Future perspective: What is the future outlook for the adoption of international labour standards? Must it be considered, first of all, that the present body of standards, consisting of area 30 instruments, how covers the essential labour problems and that the task of drawing up international standards is practically complete?

First of all, needs and conceptions change with the years at the international as well as at the national level, and the older instruments thus often have to be reworked to adopt them to contemporary needs. Already some 40 of the 150 odd Conventions were adopted of older instruments of the test of time and the lessons of experience. Whether it be a question of the earlier of social insurance which has developed into social security or of the employment of women where the concern for their protection is progressively giving way before the striving for equality. Standards are steadily being brought upto date and there is no doubt this will continue, perhaps even at an accentuated pace, in the years to come.

A second consequences of the evaluation of needs and concepts will be that new questions will arise which will call for the adoption of international labour standards. The very history of international labour law like that of national labour law— made up of the emergency of new questions as a result of social progress and of needs which make themselves felt in modern societies—the need for greater material security and welfare but also the need for freedom, equality and participation. Thus when the first ILO Convention on holidays with pay was adopted in 1936 the idea was a recent one and was considered revolutionary. Its development since is well known and what is to be said of the Convention against discrimination in employment, which was adopted in 1958, in response of relatively recent developments in ides and awareness, and which rapidly came to be regarded as one of the fundamental instruments of the ILO. In the field of occupational safety and hygiene, which affect workers lives and health rapid technological change makes necessary the constant adoption of measures against new of newly indentified risks. This trend will certainly continue. This problem of the environment will no doubt require action on a broader scale than the classical questions of occupational health and safety. Thus, again, aquaria which, although it is not new, has become more acute in modern societies has already been included in the agenda of the namely that of older workers.

These predictions are made than mere suppositions. Followings a recent "indepth review" of international labour standards, a working party of the ILO Governing Body is in the process of examining all these standards so as to identify in particular, the instruments which are in need of revision and the subjects on which the preparation of new standards should be considered. This work is still under way, but it is already apparent that the subjects which at first sight, would seem to come into these two categories are so numerous that they would fully engage all the ILO's legislative capacity for the next 25 years or more, irrespective of the question to which future developments will give rise. A huge area thus remains to be covered by international labour law, which will continue to make a major contribution to social policy in the world as long as it able to anticipate and channel the new needs of societies in constant evolution.

The continuing legislative activity gives rise to a further problem, that of the growing number of international instruments. Is there not a danger that the existence of several hundred instruments will embarrass, if not paralyse, countries (governments as well as occupational organizations)? References has some times been made to "dead wood" that needs elimination. This approach has given rise to objections that would be involved in abrogating instruments. Most of which have been the subject of formal undertakings, it has been observed that it would be unlikely that everybody would agree that a given Convention has lost all interest. While it may have become out of date for some countries, an instrument may still be of value of even premature for others. The problem is now approached from another angle, is that the working party has decided to place in a distinct category the instrument whose verification and application should be promoted on a primarily concentrated on these instruments.

A final point on which, it is possible to make a prediction without fear of error, relates to the way in which future instruments will be drafted. These is no doubt that the use of flexibility devices will be continued and even intensified, especially on Conventions laying down general principles which are supplemented by recommendations providing guidance on methods of implementation and for Conventions containing provisions for their progressive application such as those which can be ratified with the initial acceptance of only certain parts.

2.1.10 The United Nations and Human Rights

While it might have been thought that the rights of the child were adequately protected by existing human rights instruments particularly the ICCR, it was nevertheless agreed in 1799, the year of the child, that a working group of the CHR should draft a Convention which would give effect to certain child oriented right. The U.N. Convention on the rights of the child was adopted by the General Assembly in 1989 and entered into force in 1990. In addition to the protection of number of traditional civil, political, economic and social rights, the Convention includes certain rights which apply to the child alone, a child being defined by Article 2 for these purpose as every human being below the age of 18 years, unless under the law applicable to the child, majority is attained earlier. Among the 'new' rights protected are the right to a home, to know and be cared for by his or her parents, the preservation of child's identity, freedom from sexual abuse and exploitation, narcotic drugs and trafficking. A number of provisions also place obligations on appropriate measure that children will be allowed to develop their maximum potential.

Supervision under the Convention is by a ten member committee on the rights of the child. The members of the committee are to be drawn from the States parties and they serve in their individual capacities. As with other U.N. Treaties supervision is by a system of periodic reports submitted by the states parties which are studied by the committee. Under Article 45 of the Convention, the Committee is obliged to forward a biannual report of its activities to the General Assembly via ECOSOC. It is also interesting to note that UNICEF and other competent UN Organs are entitled to participate in considering the implementation of the obligations under the Convention. As yet, it is too early to speculate on the likely effectiveness of the particular area.[5]

2.2 WHO IS THE CHILD?

According to the 1989 United Nations Convention, child

5. Book—A study on behalf of the Henry Dunaut Institute—Generva. CHILD SOULDERS—The role of children in armed conflicts—Guy Goodwin-Gill and ILENE COHN.

means 'every human being below the age of 18 years unless under the law applicable to the child, majority is attended earlier'. The possibility of a patchwork definition in international law is striking and not only altogether satisfactory, as national legal systems—the applicable law, work with their effect. The age of majority is a social, religious, cultural or legal device by which societies acknowledge the transition to correction between any of the levels. For the purpose of participating in religious ritual, for example, a child may become an adult at age 13. For legal purpose, however, such as contracting obligations, including marriage, giving evidence under oath, being criminally liable or voting in elections, other age requirements will prevail. On occasion the child's actual capacity to understand will be determinative for example, in appreciating the meaning of evidence under oath, in other cases, the legislator will make assumptions as to capacity and understanding at a certain age, for example, in setting eligibility to vote.

Although State practice displays some variation, participation in the political process is nevertheless a responsibility accurate indicator of the moment at which the communities as political parties recognized the intellectual maturity of the individual. The inter-Parliamentary Union recently received the electoral system of 150 of the world's 186 Sovereign states. It noted, "The right to vote supposes that electors should have reached on age at which they are able to express an opinion on political matters, as a rule coinciding with the age of the legal majority". The name today is 'eighteen years' an overwhelming majority of 109 states has opted for this minimum age limit, with most other States having a slightly higher limit (19-21 years). The lowest limit 16 years—is practiced in four countries : Brazil, Cuba, Iran and Nicaragua.

There is again no necessary correlation in national legislation between voting age and liability to or eligibility for military service. In Brazil, Nicaragua and Iran the voting age is 16 but liability to military service starts at 19 in Brazil, 17 in Nicaragua and in subject to no apparent age limit in Iran.

Variations also occur among states as concerning 'military age', but there is as strong towards 18 or later as the minimum age for the military obligations. 185 states were surveyed and among the 103 for which information was available only 7 put the age for compulsory military service below 18 years: Afghanistan, Iran, Lao People's Democratic Republic, Mexico, Namibia, Nicaragua and South Africa; while 24 states permit voluntary enlistment of young persons below 18 years of age, generally subject to parental consent. Australia, Austria, Bangladesh, Belgium, Chile, El Salvador, Finland, Germany, Greece, Guatemala, Honduras, Iran, Libya, Luxembourg, Mauritania, Poland, South Africa, United Kingdom, United States of America and former Yugoslavia.

So far as the provisions of national laws (as opposed to actual practice) may indicate the position of States on the international laws issues attaching to requirement, a reasonable inference would support the principle of transition to adulthood at the age eighteen and the argument that young persons below that age should not be compelled to take up arms. The practice of remaining parental consent for voluntary enlistment the age of eighteen is equally consistent with such a principle.

Moreover, international humanitarian law, international human rights instruments and national legislation in numerous countries combine to prescribe the death penalty on persons under eighteen at the time of commission of the offence. This prohibition applies both in time of peace and in international and internal armed conflicts and acknowledges the reduced ability of those under eighteen to appreciate the nature of their actions in the context of criminal responsibility. The same consideration, however, is not given to the capacity of the child or young person to evaluate the reasons for death in combat.

Thus, the idea of the child as a person under 18 years enjoys a wide measure of support, even if different terminology such as 'youth' or 'young' may be a better phrase to describe those in the crucial 15-18 age bracket, whose physical and intellectual maturity is rapidly developing even as they continue to face certain legal disabilities. If age eighteen reflects a general rule, with certain limited exceptions traceable to specific, political, religious or cultural factors then the question is when and in what circumstances those under eighteen can lawfully be admitted for military service or permitted to participate in hostilities?

2.2.1 The International Law of the Child

The League of Nations adopted in 1924, the first declaration on the rights of the child, stressing the need for special care and protection. Though followed by a series of similar and related declarations, another sixty-five years were to pass before the international community acknowledgement the very special status of children and the desirability of states entering into a treaty on their behalf. The 1989 UN Convention on the rights of the child already ratified by some 144 states, is rightly recognized as a critical milestone in the legal protection of children.

At the earlier stage, in 1948, the United Nations adopted the Universal Declaration of Human Rights, a non-binding instructions since followed by both regional and global treaties in which state have accepted formal legal obligation with respect to a wide range of human rights. These include the two 1966 Covenants on civil and political rights and economic, social and cultural rights. The 1951 Convention and 1967 Protocol, relating to the status of refugees and the 1984 Convention against torture and other cruel in human or degrading treatment or punishment. All provision in these instrument pertain to children, except for specific article codifying rights of political participation extend only to those over a certain age. In addition, regional organizations have promoted local systems of obligation and supervision, for example, *the 1950 European Convention of Human Rights, the 1969 American Convention on Human Rights and 1981 African Convention on Human Rights and People's Rights*. The rules of international humanitarian law are found, in particular, in the *four* 1949 *Geneva Conventions and the two 1977* Additional protocols, as well as in the practices of States and the resolutions of the International Conference of the Red Cross and the Red Crescent.

The International law of child as a whole must be understood in context, that is as a body of rules operating primarily between States and generally having only an indirect effect only on non-state actors such as individuals, Non-Government Entities (NGEs) or other groups however do not exclude the possibility if the individual liability for beaches of the law. By contrast the international humanitarian law of internal armed conflicts applies equality to government armed forces and dissident armed group, i.e. to the 'parties to the conflict' where are gaps or contradictions as often happens when humanitarian need is opposed to military necessity, the long-standing martens clause, one of the clearest examples of a rule of customary international law in the field, recalls and confirms the most basic standard.

2.2.2 In the Words of Additional Protocols

In case not covered by this protocol or by other international agreements civilians and combatants remain under the principles of International law derived from established custom, from the dictates of public conscience.

Children, whether victims or participants in armed conflicts are thus protected and their liberties are ensured at least in theory, by international and national law. The specific provisions of international law regulating the requirements and participations of children and armed conflict turn on a number of factors, including the type of conflict and ratification of or accession to the relevant treaties. The status of the party recruiting or employing children on its ranks may also be at issue, so far as the applicability of rules other than those of international humanitarian law is concerned.

2.2.3 The Child as Protected Person

In the word of the preamble of the 1989 Convention on the Rights of the Child (CRC), 'the child should be fully prepare to live an individual life in society' and brought up in the spirit of the ideas proclaimed in the Character of the United Nations—other international instruments stress the developmental needs of the child—freedom from hunger, access to education, participation in social and cultural life—and the particular role of the family. The CRC uniquely embraces the whole spectrum of children's rights specifically endorsing the basic principles of the best interests of the child in total regime oriented to his development and self fulfillment.

2.2.3.1 Law and Process

All areas of the law would benefit from upgrading. A significant part of international human rights law is based on the protection of children and young persons up to the age of

18, a general principle which should be central to the interpretation of additional protocols I and II and the Convention on the rights of the child. So far as requirement is concerned, universal and formal acceptance of 18 as the minimum age is a key objective. International humanitarian law provides the basis for such a rule, but it needs updating and clarification. This could be promoted from the grass roots, through National Red Cross and Red Crescent Societies, with the endorsement of the Council of Delegates and the 26th International Conference of the Red Cross and Red Crescent. It must be driven too, by non-governmental organizations of all persuasions, using the resources of government, parliament, regional and international organization, the media and public support.

Specific goals should include National legislation and practice in accordance with the minimum 18 age rule, i.e. formal endorsement of the rule by the ICRC, unilateral declaration by states parties to the Convention the Rights of the Child and eventually the development of a protocol codifying the rule, the activation or improvement of existing human rights jurisdiction.

Children in internal strife, the most common situation of conflicts today, suffer because of the perceived in applicability of international humanitarian law. Every support to them should be given. Therefore, the efforts to raise the standards for example through declaration of minimum humanitarian standards they include the minimum age 18 rule and clarify the responsibilities of adults as recruiters or commanders should be made. Such an initiative also could be supported by National Red Cross and Red Crescent Societies.

The principles of the United Nations, binding upon the organization include promoting universal respect for and observance of human rights and fundamental freedoms for all without distinction as to race, sex, language or religion. The UN human rights machinery, slow as it is, must understood in the light of this overall policy goal. For example, bringing complaints to the notice of the Commission on Human Rights help it to identify situations involving consistent patterns of gross and reliably attested violation. NGOs play an important role as source of information and also in bringing such issues before the sub-commission on the protection of minorities and the prevention of discrimination so that patterns of human rights violations can be brought to the General Assembly.

UNHCR has expressly recognized its responsibilities towards children in refugee camps, who must be protected from recruitment by governments and non-governmental entities alike. The High Commissioner's reports are one way in which the problem of refugee children can be brought to the attention of a wider forum. UNHCR's strength as a human rights organization lies in the fact that it is widely represented throughout the world, particularly in areas of conflict involving both refugees and child soldiers.

UNICEF, which has a specific role under the CRC, should develop guidelines for its officials to report on recruitment and related practices, while also encouraging local NGOs to assume monitoring and reporting responsibilities.

The ICRC, although an obvious first avenue of complaint whenever a party to conflict appears to be acting in violation of its obligations under the Geneva Conventions and/or the Additional Protocols, often has very limited scope of action. The recently established *International Fact Finding Commission*, which has offered its services in the investigation of all violations of humanitarian law, including those committed in civil conflict, might be supported as a possible alternative monitoring mechanism relieving the ICRC involvement in activities that potentially compromise its impartiality.

In addition on the 'political' human rights bodies, advocates for children whether in universal or regional treaty monitoring committees offer channel for recourse, notwithstanding their particular focus and lengthy procedures.

The Committee on the Rights of the child deserves particularly close attention, specially given the number of ratifying states and the lack of provisions for derogation from the CEC. The Committee has already announced that it will develop urgent action procedures for children, draft a general comment on child recruitment and promote an optional protocol establishing minimum are 18. This Committee is also highly accessible to NGOs and by international agencies having specific responsibilities towards children, such as UNICEF and UNHCR.

2.3 WTO ON CHILDREN

The WTO grew out of the GATT-1947, which successfully developed and oversaw global trading rules in the period after the Second World War. The creation of the WTO in 1995 can be seen as the fulfillment of the vision of the participants at the Bretton Woods Conference in 1944, albeit half-a-century later. The evolution of the GATT into the WTO is aimed at reducing protectionism, reduction in tariffs and hence an increase in the world trade. The basic philosophy of the WTO is that open markets, non-discrimination and global competition in world trade are conductive to the national welfare of all countries. There has been an ever increasing realization by all countries that global governance in a rapidly integrating world economy has become important, as policies can have large and immediate detrimental effects on trade. The creation of a firm legal foundation for the institution that manages the multilateral trading system is therefore, of great importance. A stronger institution may allow the system of rules and disciplines to be enforced more rigorously than in the past and should at the very least ensure that the trade policies of the members become transparent. It would be useful to remind ourselves of the fact that GATT, however continues to exist as a substantive agreement, establishing a set of disciplines on the trade policies for its members (the other agreements, negotiated by its members are GATS and TRIPS).

The issue of standards: This has been talked of at length in the WTO standards, like regulations are technical specification for a particular product or production process. A standard differs from a regulation is that the former is voluntary, usually being defined by an industry or by a non-governmental standardization body. On other hand technical regulation are mandatory. It needs to be mentioned at this juncture that standards are usually under the control of the firms and industries. Standards whether for product or aimed at human wealth and safety, are often welfare enhancing. However, standards may have trade impeding effects which is why they are dealt within the GATT. Two basic issues need to be borne in mind first ascertaining whether a standard is indeed welfare enhancing rather than being the result of rent seeking by particular body and second the determination of the trade impact. For there to be an economic rational for standards there need to be market imperfections. The developed countries have been talking loud for the adoption of labour and environmental standards by all the trading players in the international market. There remains a requirement for interested parties to co-operate and to the extent that there are costs of developing or adhering to a standard, there may be incentive to free ride. Given that there are costs involved in meeting the standards its existence may reduce the contestability of market because potential entrants find it less attractive to compete or enter. The barriers to entry are greater and there by the profit enhancing impact of the imposition of the standards is more. Standards are thus, perceived at least by the developing partners to have created rents for the developed countries and the standard setting activity being therefore, termed as collusive.

As far as the issue of labour standards is connected, it was introduced at the insistence of the USA and France in the final stage of Uruguay round. The object of these countries was to initiate discussions on the introduction of a social clause specifying minimum standards in this area.

Talking from the view point of a developing nation, it has been suggested at various levels that the labour standards as envisaged under the WTO lend to presume that labour standards are defined to absolute and universal rather than matters to be decided by sovereign nations. It needs to be recognized that the choice standards may depend on a country's stage of development and per capita income, and therefore, the weights attached to standards may differ across welfare functions of different countries.

The social clause, is thus also aimed at forcing countries to comply with certain standards, and if the developing nations resist or fail to comply, such actions could involve imposition of import restrictions from these economies or some other type of sanction which might be even costlier to the non-complying nation. Meanwhile, it is also possible that forcing developing countries to adopt cost-raising labour standards may be harmful to their economic interests and could interface with their efforts to pursue, less interventionist and more export- oriented economic policies. Alternatively, it is also being argued that world efficiency is best served by allowing each country to set its standard in accordance with its own needs and perceptions of cost. To do otherwise, to require that all countries impose the same standards will mean that some countries impose higher standards than the corresponding social costs or that others will impose standards than the social cost. Either way outputs will then set in inappropriately low or high, as the case may be, and welfare will not be maximized.

Labour standards have emerged as a challenge in the arena of the political economy of the world trading system. In this context, it is also essential to distinguish between the difference in labour costs and differences in the labour standards. The current debate centers on the second, not the first. The reason is that labour costs are endogenous, and largely reflect a country's comparative advantage. Insisting that further trade liberlisation be mude – conditional convergence in labour costs make little sense, and would constitute blatant protectionism. The gains from trade result precisely from differences in costs, which are a reflection of differences in factor endowments and technological capacities of countries. The focus of attention is therefore, on labour standards and basic workers rights.

In the coming years, the WTO will have to face an important challenge to contain the threat of protectionist capture of the environment and labour standards issue. This may require some acceptance of harmonization through an agreement to adopt specific minimum labour standards. Some movement may be required in this direction as a *quid proquo* for further market opening in the WTO's traditional areas—goods and service markets. If, so care must be taken to minimize the possibility of capture by industrial or anti-trade lobbies. Transparency will be important here. Moreover, a necessary condition should be that affected countries are compensated for the trade barriers, except, if trade sanctions are used to enforce a multilaterally agreed treaty. Protection in such cases should not be allowed to benefit the domestic import competing industries. As the purported objective is related to labour rights, revenues collected through trade action should be used to ameliorate the situation is the exporting country.

In the fifth conference of labour minister of developing counties (1995), it was expressed that the social clause was totally unacceptable to them. In their view, it is rather imperative to commit to promote and safeguard dignity through the promotion of measures aiming at improving the working conditions of all people and provide better levels of protection.

2.3.1 United Nations Child Rights Convention: (UNCRC), 1990—A South Asian Perspective

There has been a growing awareness at the global level regarding the rights of child. Despite the growing realization world over that children must be brought up in an environment of love and care, not much headway has been made in terms of awareness about the international human rights instruments. Domestic jurisprudence must often fails, to take cognizance of the international human rights Conventions to which the respective states are a party. It is in the wider context of international human rights instruments that there is an urgent need to address the issue of children, law and justice, in the south Asian region.

There is a felt need to indicate the space available for using the United Nation's Child Rights Convention (UNCRC, hereafter) 1990, to create a legal environment favorable for the realization of the rights of children in developing countries of south Asia.

The issue of child Rights within the framework of international law, may be seen as a step ahead in the evolution of the concept of child rights within the womb of human rights and how child came to be treated as a person and how and when different efforts were initiated at the International level for a tackle of a problem of creating a suitable framework for child's rights with in the ambit of social justice. It may be noted that a historical approach towards the understanding of the development of the concept of child rights does provide some insights into the manner in which the interests of the children have come to occupy a central position in the international law. In this context, we may look at the hypothesis that the genesis of child rights cane be traced to Euro centric values and culture. The Asian children today are struggling as a result of a common legacy of authoritarianism and exploitation, which has been modified through a basic process of social, economic and legal change in Europe. The international norms on child rights are, thus as relevant for children in the western world whose societies have moved closer in this century to the egalitarian norms reflected in the various standards set by international human rights.

The framework of rights articulated in the Convention on the Rights of the child of the United Nation also, very importantly, tows the line of the basic concepts of family privacy and the role the state as parents patriae in the care and development of children. The Convention confers (a) rights of survival and development, (b) protection from abuse and exploitation, and (c) participation right; the first two fall within the traditionally accepted area of child welfare, but are given a new dimension. Although, the issues related to survival and development—the traditional areas for policy planning and intervention in many countries-have been given their due recognition, equal weight has also been given to the aspect of protection. It is important to note that there is a movement away from the perception of the child as a beneficiary of privileges conferred at the discretion of the parents, the family, the community and the state towards a perception of the child as a repository of legal rights under international law. The rights of participation incorporated in the Convention involves the development of existing legal concepts in some countries, but gives priority to the idea that children have a right to participate in matters that concern them on their community as they grow from childhood to maturity. The recognition of this concept and yet the diminishing role of parental and adult rights with, the evolving capacities of the child, introduces an important balance between familiar survival development and protection rights, and the new ideology of participation or personal autonomy rights as per the Conventions. The Convention's preamble as well as its articles confer important rights and some obligations on the child, and seek to balance them with adult rights and responsibilities.

Human rights have been perceived till now as concept that has relevance for an adult world. Critics of the Convention can argue that advocating for children will erode family values, undermind parental and family responsibility for them, and take the concept of human rights beyond its legitimate scope. However, a detailed look at the substantive article of the Convention shows that it value base prevents children's rights from being used to launch an aggressive campaign for personal autonomy so as to undermind family privacy and the role of the community and the State in the care and development of children.

An important problem relating to the UNCRC is concerned with its ratification and putting them within the legal framework of ratifying member countries. Since ratification is an executive act, there is a very real danger that the Convention will remain a treaty that does not suit local situation unless steps are taken to ensure transformation. The Indian and Sri Lankan judicial experience of treaty transformations affords some insights into the implication of legislative or political apathy in this regard. This kind of judicial activism is unusual, but it can be harnessed to ensure that a government is not apathetic with regard to its obligation to bring the legislation in a country in conformity with the Convention on the Rights of the Child. In this Context, a significant opinion that may be considered for further debates is that international instruments can themselves become part of customary law or juscogent through international consensus.

Forgoing a link with international standards through judicial activism that incorporates their norms into national law can compensate for legislative apathy in enacting laws in conformity with treaties. Monitoring and lobbying at the national and international levels combined with development assistance can be used effectively to create an environment in which States feel compelled to take initiatives to fulfil their international commitments. The status of the Convention on the Rights of the child in domestic law indicates that those who operate the legal system must be made parents in the process of implementation by combination of strategies that seek to inform advocate as well as monitor their performance on children's rights.

The UNCRC has set international standards on commitments to children that are relevant to both industrialized and developing countries. There are provisions in the

Conventions, which recognize the special problems, that developing countries face in realizing the standards set by the Convention. While the Convention envisages international co-operation and development assistance for the realization of child rights, it also encourages regional co-operation and sharing of experiences and strategies. The situation of children in the South Asian region has not improved despite several declarations and national policies and programmes. SAARC declarations have not been followed by an action plan for shared regional commitment and initiative in prioritizing the interests of children. It may thus be argued that there is a need for sharing country experience on current inadequacies in the legal systems as well as progress in the area of realizing child rights, which *interalia* can be of some relevance for national efforts to develop systems so as to obtain complements with the values and contents of the Convention.

In this context, it may be noted that the existence of personal laws in south Asia within a uniformly applicable legal regime has created problems of conflict of laws that can undermine state policies formulated by government. Pluralism can become a barrier to recognize the international standards articulated in the UNCRC, while the experience of federal of national laws and a range of different judicial and other authorities at the state of provincial levels make the task of law reform and law enforcement a complex matter. The factor of pluralism in law and the application of significant constraint as the problems of weak enforcement of laws and provision of socio-economic support do not apply for the effective realization of strategy of rights. The Convention's standards on children rights can not be realized without a serious effort to address the problem of legal pluralism in all its varying dimensions. Thus, all concerned social partners have to urgently deal on the issue of a framework for child rights within the context of the UNCRC. In fact, it may be suggested that there should be some synchronization of the upper age limit for childhood, if the rights of children are to be realized by legislation, administration, Social welfare institutions and courts of law in the 'best interest of the child' in the manner envisaged by the Convention.

As far as the acceptability among the South Asian Countries of the framework as suggested by the UNCRC is concerned the conceptual framework of the Convention with regard of the child, the family and the state is basically compatible with the values of Constitutions, Statutes and other laws in South Asia. The values in the formal legal system in areas of parental status and family relations will have to be significantly modified if the laws of these countries are to be harmonized with the conceptual framework of the Convention.

For illustrative purposes, one may consider the case of Sri Lanka and the state of Kerala in India, both of which reflect high indications of women and children in comparison of other countries in South Asia as well as other states in India. It is important to recognize that Sri Lanka and Kerala has social systems, which focused on the importance of women in the family. Legal reforms that reflect a new values system, and recognize a woman's role in the family may help to develop gender equity and strengthen the capacity of women to become agents of change and contribute to the well-being of children. Both the Conventions on the Rights of the child and the World Summit on Children contemplate development of adult literacy programmes. The commitment of the state in creating parental awareness on the rights of children, the responsibility of the family and the state so as to prevent the exploitation of children are crucial dimensions in realizing child rights in the region.

Gender equity for women cannot be realized in South Asia without addressing the basic issue of discrimination against the girl child practically in all countries. It is vital that fixed perceptions of 'paternalism' and 'protection' in linking women with children should not be allowed to undervalue the importance of making the concern with the girl child, a central issue in campaigns and strategies to realize women's rights. Establishing and developing linkages and focusing on a common agenda can help to realize substantive equality in a context where proposals for achieving formal equality may not address vital issues like the implication of child-care responsibilities within families. Besides, efforts to eliminate inequities with regard to girls may motivate political and the will of the community towards the policies that can impact on women's education and health in countries which have avoided ratification of the Convention on women's Rights.

On other positive aspects of the UNCRC, it may be noted that the cluster of articles on the right to survival and development in the UNCRC which has been described as provisional rights, aims to link the right of survival to the important right of development. The linkage is important for developing countries, in a context where invention with regard to child survival has often been seen as more basic than the right of development when a limited economic resource is available. The obligation of State parties 'to provide' for children encompasses a detailed range of measures intended to ensure that planning for survival is undertaken together with a commitment to ensure growth and development.

The Conventions perception of common and shared responsibility of parent is, therefore, not easy to realize in the context of the existing focus on pluralism in religious and customary law and including 'male breadwinner's support obligation. The reality of the common dependence of women is no argument for refusing to accept the concept of common and shared responsibility in context where the law can clarify that the contribution to child support is dependent on a parent's financial capacity or the ability to provide for a child. Reforms in the uniforms statutes, the law on support obligations of both parents, inline with the Conventions concept of family responsibility are a necessary adjunct to initiate efforts to realize the survival and development rights of children.

The need of the hour is thus, to bring into focus the debate on the child as envisaged in the UNCRC. It is, therefore, significant to note that at a time when the debt crisis and policies of structural adjustment require privatization and a movement away from public sector expansion, the provisions in the Convention play an important role for the State is ensuring that families are equipped to provide for children.

The concept of income support and State assistance to families through welfare measures can be perceived as an orthodox approach, which has been proved to be a constraint to economic growth. The losses and lack of efficiency of state enterprises has encouraged new policies in which the State moves back, and communities with employers take over the task of strengthening the capacities of the families to care for children. Community support and employer's sense of responsibility are considered adequate safety nets to achieve this task and also creative developments that will discourage welfare dependency.

Existing policies in the areas of health and education in South Asia pose the question whether the situation of families and children in particular would worsen if the existing limited state initiatives are completely replaced by a policy of non-intervention? Considering that Community and family involvement in the survival and development of children is vital, and employer initiatives are important, the question is whether the situation of children in South Asia still requires a major role of State in this regard? The Convention's articles on the relationship between the family, the state and the child envisage state involvement as well as family and community concern. Should policies in the future focus on achieving that balance or move towards non-interventions? This is an important issue which would require intense debate at all conceivable platforms.

The non-involvements of the state has an important impact on the capacity to use regulatory processes and the law in the area of rights for children. Discussions on judicial activism in the area of social and economic rights will clarify that the concept of administrative justice has been developed in the legal system of South Asia to provide relief against abuse of power of infringement of Individual rights by State officials. Constitutions have been used in recent times, especially in India, to query governmental apathy or infringement in circumstances where regulatory procedures require delivery of services to the community, and impose responsibilities for implementing a particular social and economic policy on the state. The basic Constitutional doctrine is that fundamental rights can be asserted only against the State or State agency, not against private citizens and agencies. Thus, if the states move out of this area, the legal jurisprudence on administrative matters will have to be modified significantly, if the law is to be used to contain abuse of power and inaction by private employers. This particular problem has already arisen with regard to the use of Constitutional remedies and civil action against errant employers in the investment promotion zones. Existing Constitutional provisions make it difficult to institute court action against them for violation of fundamental rights.

Activist who work in the area of women's issue child labour and occupational health are already making efforts to use even the existing law to ensure the compliance of regulatory processes by the employers. They are asking for better law enforcement, particularly in new industries in investment promotion zones, for increased converge in respect of piece rate workers and those linked to the manufacturing industry in home-based enterprises or small business. Research has revealed that worker exploitation is greatest in these small enterprises or in home-based industries, and that children have been brought into the production process at the prejudice of their schooling, even in countries where there is an effort to ensure educational participation. De-regulation and non-intervention by the state can therefore, expose children to greater risks and undermine the potential of state parties to fulfil their role under the Conventions.

While the focus on the family and the community as an important support system for its members and for family survival and development, is appropriate, the state's right and duty to strengthen families and also to penetrate in family privacy must be recognized. The concept of state performance and the state's role in relation to the family and the child that the Convention maintains requires a creative response to poverty alleviation, child protection and social security. The state's supportive role with regard to the child, the family and the community should be recognized rather than exclude giving legitimacy to interventions by the State.

Emerging trends indicate that a cutback on state support can impact on the middle income groups who are in their own way struggling to ensure the best possible care for their families and children. A 'vulnerable group' must be determined in a country's context. A failure to appreciate the need for a contextual approach can result in the marginalization of a group that is important for sustaining the very services whether it be health or education that are vital for the survival and development of all children. The phenomenon of educated migrant middle level workers from Sri Lanka and other countries being 'economic refugees' and so contributing to the brain drain of needed middle level skills is a response to the lowering of standards of living. These people are developing their own 'safety net' by seeking any job overseas. Migration of a parent or sibling becomes a strategy for economic survival of those left behind at home. Many counties in the region depend on the remittances of migrant worker as an important source of foreign exchange. The resulting social and psychological problems of these trends can create for children ethnic tensions in the host countries which indicate the vital importance of providing an adequate safety net by the state within developing counties.

It is in this context that the governments of South Asia which are pursuing new economic policies are required to reassess their own commitments with regard to allocation of resources in key areas such as education and health in order to support the families 'capacity to care for the child'. The Convention has made an important contribution in linking child development with child survival. The experience of south Asia indicates that the failure to focus on child development is a major constraint to progress on child survival. The abuses of enthusiasm with regard to non-formal education not in line with formal education has been recorded in Sri Lanka while the success of the approach in Bangladesh, indicates how low income parents perceive non-formal education positively when it feeds into the formal system. A sense that the development of the child can contribute to the child's and the family's prospects in life is a powerful motivation to ensure child survival. The experience of Sri Lanka on investment in health and education also indicates that a vision of child development which recognizes state commitments to give access to facilities for health and education to the poorest sections of society has impacted on social indicators for child survival. The investment on free education and raising literacy levels for both men and women have not raised awareness. These policies have provided a vision of different future and prospects of upward social mobility. They have helped to create a perception of the child as a valuable area rather than as another mouth to feed or another contribution to family labour in an atmosphere of grinding poverty. In emphasizing survival and development as equally important rights, the Convention encourages policy planners to perceive problems such as early marriage, denial of childhood through exploitation in the workplace and access to education as issues that are linked with child survival and ensuring adequate care, nutrition and health for infants.

The Convention on the rights of the child, despite its acceptance of progressive effort to realize economic rights depending on available resources, adopts the same 'rights' emphasis rather than a 'benefits' approach to the obligation of a state to provide for its child population. It is in this wider context that one needs to look at the scope for translating the UNCRC into specific state interventions within the national legal framework of the South Asian countries. Such an approach may be helpful to ensure the childhood of the children.

The problem of child labour has been attempted to be tackled by various legislative measures, policy interventions and other governmental initiatives, as well as those taken up by various international agencies working in this area. The recent past has been a witness to attempts and efforts to tackle this malady with a renewed vigour at all levels ranging from the grass root at the village and the Panchayat level to those by international agencies namely UNICEF and ILO (through international programmes) for the eliminations of child labour. However, while efforts are made in forms and çoverage in making a significant dent to solve the problem of child labour at international level through various agencies of U.N. there is a general feeling that most of these efforts have failed to realize the significance of convergence among those.

With a view to effectively dealing with the problem of child labour, efforts have to be made to understand its intricacies. This in turn is crucially dependent on being a able to comprehend the problem from several angle. In fact, in the absence of proper comprehension of the problem, there is a possibility that myopic actions may be taken losing sight of the multidimensional character of the problem. In such situations, the effectiveness may be lost and may be even retrograde to welfare of the children involved. A possible and realistic way of attacking the problem ought to be examined. The situation of working children in detail and the magnitude of child labour in the various parts of the country should be seen in correlation with the several ongoing development programmes in different parts of the world. This may pave the way for placing the problem in an appropriate perspective and a framework amenable to further analysis and policy formulations.

3

Labour Legislation and Protection of Children in India

India has been consistently following a proactive and child labour policy through its Constitutional provisions, legislation and administrative measures. In India, the earliest legislation which gave alleged statutory protection to the working child was the *Indian Factories Act of 1881*, which prescribed a minimum age of Seven years. Since then, successive amendments have succeeded in raising the minimum age of employment, restricting the hours to work, improving the employment conditions, and providing measures for health and safety of child labour. New areas of industrial activity have been covered through protective legislation beginning from the enactment of Mines Act, 1901 and the Employment of Children Act, 1938. After independence, the Constitution was also committed to the protection and promotion of the interest of the child which gets expression through Articles 23, 24, 39 (e) and

45. The Government of India also set-up various committees such as the *Labour Investigation Committee, 1954, Harbans Singh Committee, 1976-77, Gurupada Swamy Committee, 1979, Sant Mehta Committee, 1983 and L.M. Singhvi Committee1989.* The different committee highlighted the nature and magnitude of child labour in the different sectors which involve child labour. All the committees strongly recommended that a uniform law has to be made and a uniform age has to be fixed in order to tackle the problem of child labour. However each committee has its specific recommendations which culminated in the *Child Labour (Prohibition and Regulation) Act, 1986* which prohibits the employment of children below 14 years in certain occupations and processes.

The problem of child labour has been a world-wide problem. Industrialization on large scale leads to the employment of children in factories, workshops and other unregulated occupations. It becomes a matter of deep concern to find out ways and means which put an end to the employment and exploitation of children who are forced to join the labour stream. In recent decades, steady progress has been made in developing countries in the field of School education, resulting in a considerable improvement in the School enrolment of children. This program has especially helped in bringing down the incidence of child labour.

Adequate discussion on the status of children is significantly absent in the debates of the Constituent Assembly during the framing of the Constitutions. The reason can be that this matter might have been taken for granted during deliberations. However, when the Constitution was adopted, the preamble unequivocally states that social, economic and political justice, liberty of thought, expression, belief, faith opportunity and fraternity assuming the dignity of the individual and the unity and integrity of the nation will be secured to all the citizens. It recognizes the need for granting special protection to children. The founding fathers were wise enough to provide that the children should also have their distributive justice in future in free India. Therefore, special provisions ensuring justice to children have been incorporated in *Part III with Fundamental Rights and Part IV devoted to Directive Principles of States Policy.*

3.1 THE CONSTITUTIONAL FRAMEWORK

The Constitution of India is an elaborate document with 395 Articles which are divided into 22 parts and having 12 Schedules. It is one of the most comprehensive Constitutions in the world. This basic document of the country makes special provisions for certain selected classes of people like backward class women, children, etc. This documents even though is the supreme law of the land, it is people of India who have given to themselves this Constitution. The preamble to the Constitution states that the people of India have given to themselves the document. The Constitutional provision dealing with welfare of children are explicit and are directly categorized into two categories. The explicit provisions dealing with the child welfare are Article 15(3), 24, 39 (e) and 45. One of the important features of the Constitution of India is that while it recognizes the principle of equality before law, it provides for protective discrimination. For example, under Article 15(3) of the Constitution it is provided that State can make special provisions for women and children. Similarly, clause 4 of Article 15 allows the state to make provisions for the advancement of any socially and educationally backward classes of citizens or for the Scheduled Castes and Scheduled Tribes. Part III of the Constitution guarantees certain fundamental freedom to the citizens of the country and imposes certain restrictions on the State's power. The Constitution also authorizes the State to impose certain reasonable restrictions on the rights under third chapter. The right that are guaranteed under this chapter are;

Equality before law (Article 14)
Prohibition of discrimination on certain grounds (Article 15)
Equality of opportunity in matters of public employment (Article 16)
Abolition of title (Article 18)
Protection of certain rights regarding freedom (Article 19)
Protection against ex-post facto laws and double jeopardy (Article 20)
Protection of life and personal liberty (Article 21)

Protection against and detention in certain cases (Article 22)
Prohibition of employment of children in certain cases (Article 24)
Right of freedom of religion (Article 25)
Cultural and educational right, (Articles 29, 30) and
Right to Constitutional remedies (Article 32)

3.2 CHILD LABOUR WELFARE UNDER FUNDAMENTAL RIGHTS

Part III Constitution of India contains a long list of Fundamental Rights. This chapter has very well been described as the Magna Carta of India. Fundamental Rights are limitations upon all the powers of the government, executive as well as legislative and they are essential to the preservation of public and private rights, notwithstanding the representative chapter of political institutions. The rights are regarded as fundamental because they are most essential for the individual for the development of his full intellectual, moral and spiritual potentialities. The negation of these rights will hamper the individuals' personality development. The declaration of fundamental rights under the Constitution limits governmental activities in the interest of the liberty of the citizens. Thus children have rights to enjoy all the fundamental rights which are guaranteed to the citizens and non-citizens of India under Chapter III of the Constitution.

The guarantee of Fundamental Rights under Chapter III of the Constitution is for citizens and persons (foreigners and juristic persons). The rights to persons impliedly pave the way for protection to children in India. There are few Articles in which State in enable to protective provision in favour of children namely Articles 15(3), 24 and 39 of the Constitution.

It is submitted that a specific positive provision serves the purpose of avoiding any controversy and demonstrates the concern, however inadequate provisions of the Constitution aggravates the problem in respect of the welfare of the people including children. Our solicitude for children and repulsion for the exploitation of children of tender age compelled our founding fathers to make a specific mention of them. The State can make law for welfare of children giving them preferential treatment over other persons in the society.

Article 21 is to provide for the protection of life and personal liberty of the people including children. "Right to Life" in the context has been held to be not a mere animal existence but it is to be with human dignity and values. Article 23 of the Constitution prohibits traffic in human beings, begar and other similar forms of forced labour and exploitation. Although this article does not specifically speak of children, yet it is applied to them and is more relevant in their context because children are the most valuable section of the society. It is a known fact that many children are exploited even by the parents who allows their exploitation because of their poverty. And in the absence of parents, their exploitation by close relatives is still deeper. They are deprived of education, made to do all sorts of work injurious of their health and personality. In rural areas, children are pledged by destitute parents to the landlords as full-time servant or part time worker to look after both domestic and agricultural operation. In urban areas, the exploitation of children in myrid from exists such as helpers to artisans and skilled workers and also as domestic servants. Millions of children are exploited in violation of this fundamental right and no adequate and satisfactory legislative and administrative measures have been taken by the State to protect children.

In reference to children the word 'begar' can be given a wide cannotation. Begar does not require total absence of payment. Even inadequate payment for the work rendered by the child amounts to begar or forced labour. The most atrocious and heinous crime against helpless children is that they are captured and used by criminal gangs to indulge them in begging business. Sometimes the children of tender age are enticed for the flesh trade thus all in violation of Article 23.

Article 24 prohibits the employment of children below the age of 14 years in factories, mines or hazardous employment. But in the context of the prevailing poverty in the country, it would be extremely difficult to implement the above provision. Employment of children below a particular age is also prohibited taking into consideration their physical structure. This article does not create and absolute bar to the employment of children below the age of 14 years. Moreover it does not prohibit their employment altogether. The employment of children is prohibited only is factory or mine or in any other hazardous occupation. However, this provision is to be understood in the light of realities and economic need of parents and children in our society. As Article 24 prohibits the employment of children below the age of 14 years. It is submitted that even with respect to children above the age of 14 years, all agreements either express or implied are voidable and devoid of validity in case of exploitation. Further Article 24 is plainly enforceable against every one and reason of its compulsive mandate, no one can employ a child below the age of 14 years in a 'hazardous employment'. Hazardous employment of child below 14 years is a Constitutional prohibition which even if not followed up by the appropriate legislation, must operate with force.[1] It is therefore, necessary to identify the employment which may be called 'hazardous' employment. Thus Article 24 is an example of additional precautionary measures securing distributive justice to children.

There are also the fundamental rights which are available to any person. Thus the question arises whether the fundamental rights which are available to a 'person' are also available to the child or not? The answer to this question finds its answer whether the word 'person' includes the child or not? The Indian Constitution does not define the word 'person' obviously for child a 'person' cannot include an 'artificial person'. But the question still remains whether an unborn child is included in the definition of 'person' as used in Articles 14, 17, 18(1), 20, 21,23, 25, 27, 28 and 32 of the Indian Constitution. There is no direct decision of Indian Supreme Court on this point. The Allahabad High Court, however, held that for the purpose of section 304-A (a) of Indian Penal Code, the word 'Person' includes a child born or unborn. A child in womb can be regarded as a living entity with a life of its own. In Hindu law a child in womb is deemed to be in existence as a person is entitled to share the joint family property. Thus the fundamental rights which are available to any 'person' may also be available a child.

1. People's Union for Democratic Rights *v.* Union of India, AIR, SC 1473.

3.1.2 Child Labour Welfare Philosophy Under Directive Principles of State Policy

Part IV of the Constitution provides for certain Directives Principles of State Policy. These directions may be described as the active obligations of the State. The principles laid down are treated as fundamental in the governance of the country and it shall be the duty of the State to enforce these principles is making laws. According to Article 37, the principles provided for in Part IV are not enforceable in any court and they are to be applied by the State in making laws. The gist of this part could be laid down as follows:

> "The State shall secure a social order in which social, economic and political justice shall inform all the institutions of national life. Wealth and its source of production shall not be concentrated in the hands of the few but shall be distributed so as to subserve the common good, and there shall be adequate means of livelihood for all and equal pay for equal work. The State shall endeavor to secure the health and strength of workers, the right to work to education and to assistance in cases of want, just and humane conditions of work and living wage for workers, a uniform civil code and compulsory education for children. The state shall take steps to organize village panchayats, promote the educational and economic interest of the weaker sections of the people, raise the level of nutrition and standards of living, improve public health, organize agriculture and animal husbandry, separate the judiciary from executive and promote international peace and security, so also to foster International law and treaty obligations in the dealings of organized people with one another".

The underlying principles of the Directive Principles of State Policy are to fix certain social and economic goals for immediate attainment by bringing about non-violent social revolution. Through such a social revolution, the Constitution also seeks to achieve the objective of the child welfare. To achieve the goals of child welfare, the Directive principles of state policy have been designed with an earnest zeal to strive to promote the welfare of people by securing and protecting as effectively as it may be social order in which justice social, economical and political shall inform all the institutions of national life. Naturally, an effective implementation of this principle results in promoting the welfare of the people through social, economic and political justice and in turn is expected to promote proportionately, the child welfare also.

Article 39(e) and (f) direct the State to evolve a policy eliminating the abuse of tender age and to free children from the circumstances forcing them to enter into avocations unsuited to their age of strength. The State is also directed to create social and economical conditions and infrastructure for the healthy development of children and to provide facilities and climate for exercises of freedoms and maintenance of dignity. The State is further directed to protect the children against exploitation and moral and material abandonment.

Article 41 deals with the right to work, to education and public assistance in certain cases. Though it does not mention children. The ending words "....... and in other cases of, undeserved want". The State shall be within the limits of its economic capacity and development make effective provision for securing the right to work, to education and to public assistance in case of unemployment, old age, sickness and disablement, and in other cases of undeserved want. It covers the children as the suffering children deserved the least fate as in no cases they can he held responsible for their past sins. Hence it is the duty of State to provide social assistance to all the children who suffer for want to basic necessities of life. The implementation of this provision is also expected to promote the welfare of the children proportionately and to ensure distributive justice to them.

Article 42 requires the State to make provisions for securing just and humane conditions of work and for maternity relief. The measures for maternity relief are meant for expectant mothers during the period of pregnancy and after the child birth. These measures meant for providing proper health care and other facilities to the mothers before and after the child birth are expected to promote the health of children and to provide healthy environment for their bringing up.

Under Article 45, a duty is imposed upon the State to provide free and compulsory education within a period of ten years of the commencement of the Constitution for all the children until they complete the age of 14 years. This Directive signifies that it in not only confined to primary education, but extends to free education, whether it may be on the age of 14 years. Article 45 is thus supplementary to Article 24 on the ground that when the child is not to be employed before the age 14 years, he is to be kept occupied in some educational institution. It is suggested that Article 24 in turn supplements the clauses (e) and (f) of Article 39, thus ensuring justice to children in the matter of education. It is suggested that Articles 24 and 45 should be amended so as to raise that age limit from 14 to 16 years. By doing so the children's education atleast up to Matriculation, would be ensured for the proper growth and development of their personality. There are various State Acts, which stipulate the upper age limit of 16 years.

Article 46 provides that the State shall promote with special care, the educational and economic interests of the weaker section of the people, and in particular of Scheduled castes and Scheduled tribes, and shall protect them from social injustice and all forms of exploitation. The implementation of this principle, while promoting the economic and educational interests of the weaker section of the people particularly those of Scheduled caste and Scheduled tribes, will indirectly promote the welfare of the children of these sections of the society. The need of the welfare measures is most desirable because of the appalling poverty and backwardness of their parents.

Article 47 imposes a primary duty upon the State to raise the level of nutrition and the standard of living of its people and improvement of public health. Thus it is the responsibility of the state to provide nutritious food to the children as the word "people" includes not only adults but children as well. Perhaps this provision becomes more relevant in case of children as the malnutrition can cause irreparable danger to the personality of the children through mental retardation and blindness.

Though these directives are not enforceable by the court, yet these have been declared to be fundamental in the governance of the country. It is the obligation of the State to apply these principles in making laws. If the government ignores them it will certainly have to answer for them before the electorate at the time of the election.

Thus, it will not be correct to say that there is no sanction of enforceability behind these directives. In our democratic set-up, vigilant public opinion is the real force behind the political institution which stands for the benefit of individual. The actions of the government are subject to security by the masses and distinguished leader of the different parties. If the government pursues a policy in accordance with the principles of the Constitution, people tolerate it, otherwise they oust it in the next election. Since these directives relating to the welfare of children have also been embodied in the Constitution the government is apt to implement them. Through they do not have legal force behind them but the highest tribunal, i.e. public opinion is behind them.

According to interpretation given by the Supreme Court in earlier cases to Article 37 and IV, these directions even it disobeyed by the state, could not affect the legislative power of the state. This approach was due to the stand that these directives are only directory in scope and operation. However, there was a substantial change in this judicial attitude and recent decisions project this view. In *Air India Statutory Corporation* v. *United Labour Union*,[2] the Supreme Court reiterated that Directive Principles in the Constitution are forerunners of the U.N. Convention on the Right to Development as inalienable human right and every person and all people are entitled to participate in, contribute to, and enjoy, economic, social, cultural and political development in which all human rights and fundamental freedoms would be fully realized. These principles are regarded as embedded as integral part of the Constitution in the Directive Principles. Therefore, these principles now stand elevated to inalienable fundamental human rights. Even though earlier the Directive Principles were considered to be non-justiciable they are regarded as justifiable by themselves. Another important landmark in the Indian Constitution in Article 141 which proclaims that "the law declared by the Supreme Court shall be binding on all Courts within in territory of India. Hence even in the absence of a

2. AIR 1997, SC, 645.

specific law if the Supreme Court declares the law, it will be binding on all courts in the country.

Cases like *Mohini Jain* v. *State of Karnataka*,[3] *Unni Krishan* v. *State of Andhra Pradesh*[4] *and M.C. Mehta* v. *State of Tamil Nadu*[5] are example in this regard.

3.2 PROTECTIVE LEGISLATIONS FOR CHILD LABOUR IN INDIA

After the freedom of the country, special and protective legislations have been made for children in India. Because of their tender age, weak physique, inadequately developed mind and understanding, they need protection against moral and physical harm as well as exploitation by others. In the formative years of their life, they need special care service to realize full potential for growth and development. There are about 300 Central and State Statutes concerning children. These have been enacted with an intention to protect and help children to achieve the goal of child labour welfare enshrined in our Constitution.

To prevent employment of children in occupations hazardous for their health and to regulate the working conditions in different sectors of employment many legislations have been passed from time to time. However, something is yet to be done to solve the problem, i.e. efficient enforcement of legislations without any deficiency. This is more in case of child labour particularly in the unorganized sector. This fact has been admitted by various committees under government control from time to time.

3.2.1 Historical Retrospect of Protective Legislations

The first protective legislation for child labour in India was seen in 1881 in the form of *Indian Factories Act* which had the provisions prohibiting employment of children below 7 years, limiting the working hours for children to 9 hours a day and providing 4 holidays in a month and rest hours. This was actually made by the ruling British Government to decrease the production in Indian industries through some legal restrictions.

3. AIR 1992(3), SCC, 666.
4. 1993(1), SCC 645.
5. 1995(6), SCC, 756.

It may be submitted that the labour legislations in India including protective legislation for children have been greatly influenced with the result of various Conventions and Recommendations adopted by International Labour Organisation. Besides Constitutional provisions there are several legislative enactments which provide legal protection to children in various occupations.

The Children (Pledging of Labour) Act, 1933,
The Employment of Children Act, 1938,
The Minimum Wages Act, 1948 and rules made thereunder by the government,
The Factories Act, 1948,
The Plantations Labour Act, 1951,
The Mines Act, 1952,
The Merchant Shipping Act, 1958,
The Motor Transport Workers' Act, 1961,
The Apprentices Act, 1961,
The Atomic Energy Act, 1962,
The Beedi and Cigar Workers (Conditions of Employment) Act, 1966,
The Shops and Establishment Act in Various States, and
Child Labour (Prohibition and Regulation) Act, 1986.

An attempt is made to trace the evolution of the present law through the years under different enactment. Legislative response in this regard like the other areas in labour laws is being criticized in many circles as *ad-hoc* and very often half-hearted. Industrialization brought with it several woes for the working class especially long hours of work from dawn to dusk, which got extended with the invention of electric bulbs. The fate of the children was also not different where they used to accompany the parents to the work place. *The Child Labour (Prohibition and Regulation) Act*, 1986 was the culmination point of the following legislative landmarks:

1881 : The Factories Act

(a) Factories employing 100 or more persons were covered by this Act.

(b) Minimum age of a child employment was fixed as seven years.
(c) Successive employment for the same employee, i.e. employment in two factories on the same day was prohibited.
(d) Working hours was prescribed not to exceed nine hours a day and at least four holidays to be given in a month.

1891 : The Factories Act (Received)

The Act was revised with respect to the following matters:

(a) Minimum age was increased to 9 years.
(b) Hours of work was limited to maximum seven hours per day, with prohibition of work at night between 8 p.m. and 5 a.m.

1901 : The Mines Act

The Act Prohibited the employment of Children under 12 years of age.

1901 : The Factories Act

This Act Prohibited work of children between 7 p.m. and 5.30 a.m. it also provided for :

(a) Work in certain dangerous processes prohibited.
(b) Certificate of age and fitness required.

1922 : The Factories (Amendment) Act

To implement the ILO Convention (No. 5) 1919, the Factories Act was amended in 1922 which provided for the following changes:

(a) Minimum age-limit was increased to 15 years.
(b) Reducing the working hours to a maximum of 6 hours, and also an interval of half an hour was provided for if children who are employed for more than 5½ hours.
(c) Scope of the Act was limited to establishment employing 20 or more persons with mechanical

processes, with power given to the local government to exclude the provisions to premises employing 10 or more persons.

(d) Prohibition of employment of children below 18 and women in certain processes.

(e) Provision for medical Certificate plus Certificate of re-examination for continuing work.

1923 : The Indian Mines Act

This Act prescribed a higher minimum age for employment in mines i.e. from 12 to 13 years.

1926 : The Factories (Amendment) Act

This amendment imposed certain penalties on the parents and guardians for allowing their children to work in two separate factories on the same day.

1931 : The Indian Ports (Amendments) Act

This Amendment provided that 12 years shall be the minimum age of a person for handling goods in ports.

1931 : The Report of the Royal Commission on Labour

The Commission and its recommendation had and impact on legislation pertaining to child labour during the period 1931 to 1949.

1932 : The Tea District's Emigrant Labour Act

This Act was passed to check migration of labourers to districts like Assam. It also provided that no child should be employed or allowed to migrate unless the child is accompanied by his parents or an adult on whom the child is dependent.

1933 : The Children (Pledging of Labour) Acts

This Act Prohibited pledging of children i.e. taking of advances by parents and guardians in return for bonds, pledging the labour of their children—a system akin to that of the present day bonded labour system. This practice of pledging of labour of children was found to be prevalent in areas such as Amritser, Ahmedabad, Madras, etc., in carpet and bidi factories by the Royal Commission. The children in these situations were found to be working under extremely unsatisfactory working conditions. Hence, the Royal Commission recommended that the expediency of penalizing the giving of advances to secure the labour of children and that the bond for pledging the labour of a person under 15 years executed on account of any consideration should be void, as was observed by the Commission. The System is indefensible, it is worse than the system of indentured labour is, when he enters on the Contract, a free agent while the child is not.

This recommendation was given effect to by the legislature by introducing in the legislative Assembly a Bill called the Children (Pledging of Labour) Bill in 1932 which was a year later converted into an Act.

1934 : The Factories (Amendment) Act

This amendment Act had elaborate provisions for regulating the employment of children of various age groups with regard to factories, such as :

(a) Children under 12 and 15 employment generally prohibited.

(b) Children between 12 and 15 years employment restricted to 5 hours a day.

(c) Children between 15 and 17 years certain restrictions on employment were imposed.

1935 : The Mines (Amendment) Act

This amendment introduced divisions of children according the age groups and the following restrictions were introduced:

(a) Employment of children under 15 years in mines was prohibited.

(b) Underground employment of persons between 15 to 17 years was permitted only on production of certificate of physical fitness granted by a qualified medical practitioner.

(c) Working time restricted to Maximum 10 hours a day and 54 hours a week for above the ground and 9 hours a day for work underground.

1938 : The Employment of Children Act

This Act was passed to implement the Convention adopted by the 23rd Session of ILO (1937) which inserted a special Article for India, that :

> "Children under the age of 13 years shall not be employed or work in the transport of passengers, or goods, or mails, by rail, or in the handling of goods at docks, quays of wharves, but excluding transport by land. Children under the age of 15 years shall not be employed or work in occupations to which this Article applies which are scheduled as dangerous or unhealthy by the Competent authority".

Hence it :

(a) Prohibited the employment of children under 15 years in occupations connected with transport of goods, passengers, mails or railways.
(b) Minimum age for handling goods on docks was raised from 12 to 14 years.
(c) Requirement of Certificate of age.

1948 : The Factories Act

An entirely new Act consolidate and amend the law relating to labour in factories was passed in 1948 and it came into force on April 1, 1949. By 1948 Act, it was tried to implement as many of the provisions of ILO, Code of Industrial Hygiene as they were practicable under India conditions. The Provisions relating to Periodical Medical Examination of young persons was made. This provision widened the definition of the "factory" and abolished the distinction between seasonal and non-seasonal factories. It raised the minimum age for admission of children to employment from 12 to 14 years and reduced the maximum permissible daily hours of work of children from 5 to 4 hours and a half.

The Employment of Children Act, 1938 (Act 26 of 1938)

The Act was passed to combat the evil of child labour in workshops. This Act was amended in 1939, 1948, 1949 and 1951.

The main object was to check the abuses arising out of the employment of children in workshops which were outside the scope of factories legislation. It wanted to regulate the employment of children in occupation connected with :

(a) Transport of passengers, goods or mails.
(b) In port authority.

The employment of children below the age of 15 in any occupation connected with the transport of passengers etc. as noted above was completely prohibited. It further laid down that with the exception of children employed as apprentices or trainees, no child between the ages of 15 and 17 years, would be employed or permitted to work in these occupations unless he was allowed a rest interval of at least 12 consecutive hours in a day which was to include the period between 10.00 p.m. and 7.00 a.m. Only the Government could relax this restriction in case of an emergency.

This Act forbade the employment of children below 14 years in the workers connected with beedi-making, carpet weaving, cement manufacture (including bagging of cement), cloth printing, dyeing and weaving, manufacture of matches, explosive and fire works, cutting and splitting and shellac manufacture, soap manufacture, tanning and wool cleaning. The State Government had legislative authority to extend these provisions to other employments also. Accordingly transport workers in Tamil Nadu and brassware and glass bangles industries in Uttar Pradesh.

Under this Act, the Railways and port required to maintain registers showing the names and dates of births of children below the age of 17 years employed by them. Their periods of works, intervals of rest, nature of work, etc., and notices to that effect were to be displayed. Contraventions were made penal offences. Almost all the State Govts., and also Railways and Port authorities framed rules under this Act.

The Employment of Children Act, 1938 was repealed by the Child Labour (Prohibition and Regulation) Act, 1986

Under this Act, Some procedure was laid down for the first time in which employment, occupation or processes, the employment of children should be banned. Again for the first time some regulatory provisions were laid down in respect of the working conditions of children in most of the employments where they were not prohibited from working. This Act, by way of amendment, redefined the definitions of 'adolescent', 'adult', and 'child' in the *Minimum Wages Act, 1948, Plantations Labour Act, 1951, Merchant Shipping Act, 1958 and Motor Transport Workers' Act, 1961.*

The Motor Transport Workers Act, 1961 (27 of 1961), as amended in 1986

The Act was passed to regulate the condition of service of motor transport workers. In such Act "a child" means, a person who has completed the fourteenth year and "adolescent" means a person who has completed his fourteenth year but has not completed his eighteenth year. Chapter VI of such Act regulates the employment of young persons, i.e. the children and the adolescent. This Act provides for penalty and procedure for prosecution for violation of such statutory provisions.

It was noticed that a sizeable number of child workers being engaged in the beedi and cigar manufacturing units and also in motor transport concerns were being forced to work under most unhealthy and unhygienic conditions. *The Beedi and Cigar Workers (Conditions of Employment) Act, 1966 (32 of 1966)* was enacted for regulating the conditions of their service. Ten years there after, i.e. in 1976 the *Beedi Workers Welfare Cess Act and Beedi Workers Fund Act were passed.*

Mining Legislation

Indian Mines Act (8 of 1901) was passed in 1901. The Chief Inspector was granted power to prohibit employment of children. (as also women) in mines where the conditions were dangerous to their health and safety. This Act was replaced by the Indian Mines Act, 1923 (4 of 1923), in which the definition of "Child" was amended to mean a person under the age of thirteen years. Under this Act no child could be employed in a mine or to be present in any part of mine which was below the ground or in any open excavation in which any mining operation was being carried on.

By 1935 amendment of the Indian Mines Act, the minimum age for employment of children in mines was raised from thirteen to fifteen years. An adolescent (i.e. between 15 and 17 could be employed underground only when he had been duly certified by a qualified Medical practitioner.

In order to update the mines legislation, at par with the Factories Act, the Mines Act was re-enacted in 1952. It provided for severe punishment including imprisonment for contravention of the provisions of the Act. Minimum age for employment below ground was raised to 18 years. An interval of rest of half an hour after every 4½ hours of continuous work was provided with. An adolescent could not be employed in any mine expect between 6.00 a.m. and 6.00 p.m.

Mines Act was amended by the Act No. 62 of 1959 (w.e.f. 16-1-1960) and then substantially by the Act No. 42 of 1983 (w.e.f. 31-5-1984). Present position is that under S-40 no person below eighteen years of age can be allowed to work in any mine or any part thereof. Only trainees and apprentices, not below sixteen years of age, may be entertained after prior approval of the Chief Inspector or Inspector. Contravention of this provision is a penal offence, vide Section-68. A person below eighteen years of age cannot even be allowed to be present in any part of a mine. Vide Section 45.

Plantation Legislation

Plantation legislation grew with cultivation of tea in Assam and Dooars owing to scarcity of workers in those regions, they were being brought from other parts of the country. Understandably, early legislations were proplanters.

To name a few:

(a) The Workmen's Breach of Contract Act, 1859 (VII of 1859).
(b) The Employment and Workmen's (Disputes) Act, 1860 (IX of 1860).
(c) Indian Penal Code 1860.
(d) The Assam Labour and Emigration Act, 1901 (VI of 1901).

(e) The Madras Planter's Act, 1903 (Provided with penal measures to protect the planners from loss of advances to the workers).

(f) The Jalpaiguri Labour Act, 1912.

(g) The Coorg Labour Act, 1926 (Provided with penal measures like the Madras Planter's Act).

Most of the above legislations were put to end in course of time. On the basis of recommendations of the Royal Commission on Labour the Tea Districts Emigrant Labour Act was passed in 1932 (XXII) of 1932 for (i) free movement of labour, and (ii) greater security for labourers. Under this Act children under 16 could not be migrated to tea plantation areas unless accompanied by parents or guardians. Curiously enough, this Act did not contain any provision regulating wages, hours of work, accommodation sanitation, water supply, educational facilities, recreation, etc. As the title suggested, it was substantially a statute on emigration.

Finally, the Plantation Labour Act, 1951 (LXIX of 1951 came into being after considerable deliberations. Its provision on conditions of work and employment were largely made similar to those of the Factories Act. The State Governments were empowered to make rules on welfare measures. Rules could be so made for providing with recreational facilities for worker's children and where there were more than 25 children of the worker's between the ages of 6 and 12 to provide with educational facilities.

This Act fixed the weekly working hours for children and adolescents at 40 and prohibited employment of children under 12 years of age. A certificate of fitness by surgeon was necessary for employing a child or an adolescent who did not complete the age of 15 years and 18 respectively. Except with the State Government's permission no child worker could be employed between 6.00 a.m. and 7.00 p.m.

The Act made provisions for annual leave with wages for a child or adolescent worker one day for every 15 days of work. Such leave could be accumulated for 30 days. Adequate penal measures were provided with for non-observance of such provisions made under the Act/Rules framed thereunder.

Paradoxically, many of such legal measures could not be translated into action because of slump tea industry which started towards the end of the year 1951. As a result, the Act was enforced only on April 1, 1954. *The Plantation Labour Act was amended by Act No. 42 of 1953, Act No. 34 of 1960, Act No. 33 of 1961, Act No. 58 of 1981 and Act No. 61 of 1986.* Under 1986 amendment the "adult" would mean a person who has completed his eighteenth year, an "adolescent" would mean when he completes fourteenth year but not eighteenth year and "child" would mean when he has not completed his fourteenth year.

Other Legislations

The Merchant Shipping Act, 1958

The Act prohibits employment of children between the age 15 years in any capacity on sea going ships except (a) in a school-ship or in a training ship or (b) in a ship in which all persons employed are members of one family, or (c) in a home-made ship of less than two hundred tons gross or (d) where such person is to be employed on nominal wages and will be in the charge of his father or other adult near male relatives.

The Inland Stream-Vessels Act, 1917

It does not contain any provision on the employment of child-worker. Children below 18 years of age are prohibited to be employed at a place where radiation takes place under *the Radiation Protection Rules, 1971. The States have statutes under the title State Shops and Commercial Establishment Act* which regulates employment of children in shops, restaurants and hotels, etc. where the Factories Act, 1948 does not apply. Thus the minimum age of employment in shops and commercial establishments is 12 years in Bihar, Gujarat, J&K, Madhya Pradesh, Karnataka, Orissa, Rajasthan, Tripura, U.P., West Bengal, Goa, Daman and Manipur and 14 years in Andhra Pradesh, Assam, Haryana, Himachal Pradesh, Kerala, Tamil Nadu, Punjab, Delhi, Chandigarh, Pondicherry and Meghalaya. The minimum age of employment is 15 years in Maharashtra.

The Child Labour (Prohibition and Regulation) Act, 1986

This is an Act to prohibit the engagement of children in certain employments of hazardous nature and to regulate the conditions of doing work for the children in certain other employments of non-hazardous nature. It replaced the Employment of Children Act, 1938, but reproduces its schedules A and B. The Act consists of four parts. Part I contains definitions. Part II deals with the prohibitions of employment of children in certain occupations and processes. Part III regulates child labour in those establishments where children under 14 may be permitted to work namely those establishments where none of occupations or processes of Schedules A and B are carried on Part IV lists the penalties for violations of the Act.

Though the previous Acts prohibit the employment of children below 14 and 15 years in certain specified employments, there was no procedure laid down in any law for deciding in which employment, occupations or processes the employments of children should be banned. There was also no law to regulate the working condition of children in most of the places where they are not prohibited from working and were working under exploitative conditions. The present Act:

(a) bans the employment of children, i.e. those who have not completed their 14th year, in specified occupations and processes,

(b) lays down a procedure to decide modifications to the Schedule of banned occupations or processes,

(c) regulates the conditions of work of children in employment where they are not prohibited from working,

(d) lays down enhanced penalties for the employment of children in violation of the provisions of this Act, and other Acts which forbid the employment of children, and

(e) brings about uniformity in the definition of "child" in related laws.

No fundamental changes have been incorporated in the 1986 Act and in most essential matters it is a replica of the old Employment of Children Act, 1938. By defining child as a person who has not completed his or her 14th year of age in section 2(ii), the Act reduces a child from 15 years to 14. The Constitutional benckmark of 14 years was used to lower the age from the higher age for the protection of the child. This permits more children to be employed in the areas of merchant shipping and motor transport. Here the Constitution has been used by the parliament and government to take away the protection of children between 14 and 15.

The definition of "establishment" in Section 2(iv) lacks clarity if the term includes, or would include in course of time, some of the activities in which child labour need to be protected. The present definition is likely to pave the way for the orgnised sector or units to deploy children in sub-human conditions. Though the present Act does not ban child labour in the family, the only difference is that it restricts the definition of the family to include the parents, children, brothers and sisters in Section 2(v) as against the broader definition of section 3(iii) of the 1938 Act. The word "occupier" in section 2(vi) is not clearly defined and, therefore, may not check employers agents and contractor, who play a vital role in the employment of children.

The Provision of Section 3 keeps any occupation, a work or process, i.e. carried on by the occupier with the aid of his family—out of the purview of the Act. This provisions offers protection to several match, carpet, glass and bidi manufacturing units to continue the exploitation under the umbrella of the family. Therefore, there is a need to add to the provision that "it shall be presumed that the occupier is also the employer for the purpose of the Act and shall be liable for prosecution". The onus to prove that the child is a member of his or her family would rest on the occupier. Though the provision says that nothing in this section shall apply to any workshop where any process is carried on by the occupier with the aid of his family or to any school established by, or receiving assistance or recognition from the government, when certain occupations and processes are harmful of the health of children, it remains applicable even if children work as part of family enterer rises, or state managed/established/added/recognized schools. Once the occupations/processed have been identified as hazardous for the employment of children, any exemption made thereof is to the detriment of the children. Can thereby any justification for such exemption?

Along with the prohibited occupations and processes which the 1938 Act listed, the new Act includes the prohibition of work in the building and construction industry after the Supreme Court order in 1981. Work relating to the selling of crackers and fire works in shops with temporary licenses was added to the list of occupations along with the manufacture of slate pencils (including packing). Manufacture of products from agate and processes using toxic metals and substances such as lead, mercury, Manganese, Chromium, Cadmium, Benzene, Pesticides and Asbestos were inserted in the list of hazardous processes respectively by *Notification No. S.O. 404 (E) dated 5 June 1989, published in the Gazette of India.*

The Act does not include balloon and other factories where children are forced to work with fire and dangerous chemicals. It is also silent on children working in the agricultural sector which constitutes 80% of child employment.

The word 'hazardous' is not clearly defined in this Act and it is left to the Technical Advisory Committee to define hazardous occupations and processes. Also there is no provision in the Act to seek the prohibition of child labour in an occupation or a process even if the request is backed by relevant data, and no fixed time to respond to such a request. Therefore, it is necessary that the Central Government takes up the task of revising the definition of 'occupations' and 'processes' for the purposes of making additions to the schedule in time-bound and planned manner.

With modernization and rapid industrialization along with tremendous strides in electronics, can one really precisely define what is hazardous and what is not within definite time frames? More and more hazardous jobs for children will make the scene in time. Some jobs which are not hazardous today will become hazardous tomorrow. Besides, the adjective "hazardous", is held to have purely physical implication excluding the psychological, mental and emotional danger that a job can mean to child workers in any given work. The very fact that childhood is snatched from a child and it is forced to experience an adulthood, it is not prepared for, transforms every aspect of what should be an optimistic environment for a child into a pessimistically hazardous one. Moreover, the present Act does not specify the minimum age of employment of children in occupations and processes other than the prohibited ones.

The present Act legalizes the entry of children in hazardous occupations by regulating their development in industries that are obviously non-hazardous for adult but are hazardous for children. Another significant aspect of the 1986 Act on the more stringent punishment for violations under section 14 which ranges from a fine of Rs. 10,000 to 20,000 or a minimum of three months imprisonment to a maximum of one year or a combination of both fine and imprisonment.

However, one should understand that the earlier Acts were flawed not because the penalties were too light but because they were rarely enforced. It is necessary that the penal provisions be excluded from the purview of operation of the provisions of the first offenders Act by inserting a specific clause to this effect that offences under the present Act be made cognizable. Besides, offences made in any Act involving child labour should be deemed to be an offence under the *Child Labour (Prohibition & Regulation) Act, 1986,* by inserting suitable provisions in this and other Acts.

3.2.2 National Policy on Child Labour

The implementation of child labour legislation in our country is very ineffective during last five decades. The main reasons for this are lack of adequate enforcement machinery, lack of political will, deliberate attempt to employers to flout the legal provisions and the lack of consciousness within the minds of parents themselves who obtain false age and medical certificates to enable their children to work in different undertakings. The number of labour inspectors as enforcement offices is far from the satisfaction. They can barely visit all the factories in their jurisdiction. Keeping in view the pitiable conditions of child labour in India, the Government of India has endeavored to expand national policy on child labour welfare. New projects are on the anvil for regulating child labour in our country.

I. The Constitution of India in the Directive Principles of the State Policy and as a part of the Fundamental

Rights, has laid down that the State shall direct its policy towards securing that health and strength of workers, men and women, and the tender age of children particularly be given opportunities and facilities to develop in a healthy manner and in conditions of freedom and dignity. Childhood and youth are to be protected against exploitation and no child below the age of 14 years shall be employed to work in any factory or mine or engaged in any other hazardous employment.

II. The National Policy for Children Resolution, adopted in August 1974, further develops adequate services for children. These were to form a prominent part of the nation's plan for development of human resources. Free and compulsory education for all children up to the age of 14, provision of health and nutritional programmes and services, providing alternative forms of education for children unable to take full advantage of formal school education for whatever reasons and measures for protecting children against neglect, cruelty and exploitation form part of the National Policy for Children. The policy also provides, as one of its objectives, that permitted to be engaged in hazardous occupation or to be made to undertake heavy work.

III. *The Committee on Child Labour (Gurupada Swamy Committee)* which submitted its report in December, 1979 examined the problems of child labour in detail. India is one of countries where the problem of child labour is quite openly manifest and the widespread existence of child labour has been viewed by the Government of India with concern. The Gurupada Swamy Committee recognized that a distinction has to be made between child labour and the exploitation of child labour as, through both are a problem, they are of different orders, it has underlined that in full future action dealing with child labour, this basic aspect would have to taken, i.e. "Labour become an absolute evil in the case of the child when he is required to work beyond his physical capacity, when hours of employment interfere with his education, recreation and rest, when his wages are not commensurate with the quantum of work done, and when the occupation he is engaged endangers his health and safety, i.e. when he is exploited.

IV. Government has given consideration to these aspects of the problems of child labour, i.e. the need to protect child labour from exploitation or from being subjected to work in hazardous conditions, which endanger such chidren's physical and mental development; the need to ensure safety and health at their working places; that they should be protected from excessive long working hours and from night work, and that should be regulated work even in non-hazardous occupations; and that all child labour have to be provided with sufficient weekly rest periods and holidays in their employments.

V. The recently enacted Child Labour (Prohibition and Regulation) Act, 1986, is the culmination of the process of consideration that Government has given to this pervasive problem figuring in the economic and social landscape in the country. Both, in enacting the legislation, and thereafter in proceeding to lay down the policy, the outline of the policy and the outline of the programme of action, Government has to keep in mind the economic and social aspects of child labour in the country. For example, with substantial portions of Gross Domestic Product (GDP) coming from the agricultural sector, rural industries or artisans, workshops, or small scale services, often children work as an essential part of a farm household, or as part of the working family assisting parents in ancillary tasks. In such working activities by children in farm and field, in artisan households or in small family-centered trade or service establishments, children most often acquire the skills which enable them to become full-fledged workers in farming households, family establishments or trade. While work of such kinds has its problems, it is more essential at the present stage of national development to concentrate in those sectors or establishments where children are deployed on wage or quasi-wage employment, outside the family, where there is most likely to arise exploitation in whatever form it may be.

VI. The National Anti-poverty policies, the National Education policy, the National policy on Health for all and on Nutrition as also the generally stepped up provisions in social services in national plan outlays, are all geared to tackle the problems of poverty, where too often the origins and compulsions of child labour are rooted. The general raising of large numbers of the population above the poverty line, or the provision of the entire spectrum of improved social services in the above-mentioned areas will, it is hoped, lead to progressive elimination of poverty, and consequently of the phenomenon of children being put out of wage employment of quasi-wage employment at unsuitable ages. The measures to promote employment-oriented development, both in rural and urban areas, and the all-round development and extention of adequate facilities for both formal and non-formal education, vocational education and training and in the coverage and extension of social security and family welfare measures would all go a long way to tackle the basic and root causes of child labour.

VII. This action programme, therefore, has to be viewed against the above-background specifically, the attempt is to deal with a situation where children work, or compelled to work, on a regular or a continuous basis to earn a living for themselves and/or for their family, and where their conditions of work result in their being severely disadvantaged and exploited, and where abuses connected with such factors impacting on wage-employed children need to be given close attention by the State for rectification, amelioration and regulation through specific legal and administrative instruments and measures.

VIII. The future action programme is setout under the following three heads:

(a) The legislative Action plan,
(b) The focusing of general development programmes for benefiting child labour, wherever possible, and
(c) Project-based plan Action in areas of high concentration of child labour engaged in wage/quasi wage employment, legislative Action plan.

3.2.2.1 Legislative Action Plan

I. A child Labour *Technical Advisory Committee* has been setup to advise the Central Government on addition of occupations and process to the schedule contained in *the Child Labour (Prohibition and Regulation) Act, 1986* (hereinafter referred to as CLA, 86).

II. The provision of the CLA, 86, the Factories Act and the Mines Act will be enforced so as to particularly ensure that children are not employed in factories or mines or in any hazardous employment, and where they are employed in non-hazardous employments or occupations, to ensure that the work is regulated in accordance the Part III of the CLA, 86. Where it is necessary for State Governments to make rules under CLA, 86, or under any other legislation so as to protect the interest of child labour, they will be so requested to undertake review and frame rules as necessary. The Railway administration, Major ports and Central and State Government departments, incharge of oilfields and mines will also similarly be asked to review the situation arising from the enactment of CLA, 86, so as to ensure that child labour is not employed in prohibited occupations or employments, that the provisions setout for their health and safety, for the maintenance of registers, and for regulating the periods and days, of rest are enforced in all establishments.

III. Governments will also bring forward legislation to delete the provision contained in the Minimum Wages Act, allowing different to be fixed for children, adolescents and adults. In other words, children will have to be paid the same as adults. This will remove the economic incentive to employ child labour on lower wages. For enforcing other protective legislations like the *Payment of Wages Act, the Equal Remuneration Act*, etc., it will be ensured that child labour is not discriminated against as compared to adult labour. The Central and State Inspection machinery will be geared up for this purpose.

3.2.2.2 Focussing of General Development Programmes for Benefiting Child Labour

National Development programmes exist with very wide coverage in areas of education, health, nutrition, intregrated child development and the anti-poverty group of programmes. In order to have an impact on child labour, it will be necessary to focus these programmes by the implementing agencies under the State Governments or the Central Government, so as to deliver benefits to child labour whenever possible. Some areas where such focusing could be possible are set out below:

(a) *Education* : The National Policy on Education, 1986 (NPE) sets the target of all children who attain the age of 10 years by 1990 having had five years of schooling or its equivalent, through a non-formal education (NFE) centers proposed to be opened, which will supplement the formal education system. Since the central feature of the implementation of the strategy for non-formal education is based on micro-level and area specific and population specific planning. NFE Centers for child labour will be set-up with the involvement of voluntary agencies and *Panchayati Raj* Institutions which are capable of running non-formal education centers, wherever possible, to cater to child labour who, after work or during holidays, can present themselves at the NFE Centers. Special attention will be given to attracting and retaining girls from working children to NFE Centers. Part-time courses and vocational courses will also be catered to all these centers. Such non-formal education up to class VIII level children up to class V level, with arrangements for continuance of non-formal education up to class VII level, wherever possible, to organize such NFE centers for child labour, all the special features figuring in the programme of action of the NPE will be provided.

(b) For child labour belonging to disadvantaged classes like SC/ST families, details of a scheme of incentive/ assistance to indigent SC/ST families who have to put out their children to wage/quasi-wage employment, will be worked out in consultation with State Governments. For such children who come from families engaged in occupations like scavenging, with constant micro-planning needs verification to ensure that SC/ST Child Labour enrolled in Non-formal Education centers successfully the course of non-formal education up to class VIII. These are as per the specific provisions laid down in the programme of action of the NPE.

(c) Micro-Planning for non-formal education centers will have to be undertaken for child labour, especially for those belonging to such disadvantaged sections of the society as SC/ST, or in areas where there is high concentration of such disadvantages groups of families.

(d) In urban areas also especially in urban slums, non-formal education programmes by both the State Governments and by voluntary agencies will be promoted, including the organization of extracurricular activities, diversity in learning activity and with a provision of games and sports and related equipments plays and skills, excursions, etc.

(e) The projects of voluntary agencies will be entertained for a period of 3-4 years, whether for urban or rural areas, and while the initial proposals would be required to be sent to the State Governments, at subsequent stages, the voluntary agencies will directly approach the Department of Education for release of grants-in-aid to such non-formal education centers. The Ministry of Labour, Govt. of India may also arrange for micro-level help of Department of Education.

(f) NRE/RLIGP funds would be used on a priority basis for creating the infrastructure for Non-Formal Education Center catering to child labour under the overall co-ordination and direction of the local district level development authorities.

(g) For continuing education of child labour who have been enrolled and successfully completed their period of non-formal education efforts would be made to link the non-formal educational institutions with the open schools, or with the formal educational system, so as to enable them to continue their education. The non-formal education progaramme would also be linked with the *Shiksha Nilayams* and vocational and technical courses of a wide variety would be provided where required for among others, working children who come from the non-formal stream.

(h) *Health*: Health is a State subject and the progranmme of medical inspection of children have been assigned to the States. The progress among the various states is uneven. A few States have good programmes, but many other States do not. Those States where there exists a school health service programme are many and in some states even all, primary school going children in the rural areas have been covered under scheme for regular examinations. But those children who do not join school because of being at work would obviously not be covered by such school health programmes (where they exist). The Ministry of Health and Family Welfare, Govt. of India will address the state Governments, recommending that intensive medical inspection of children be taken up in those areas where child labour is prevalent. The State Governments will have to be persuaded to extend the coverage of the school health services programme to child labour. Since this is an area essentially under the State sector, a continuing dialogue, effort and persuasion with the State Governments will have to be maintained, so that all children irrespective of whether they are in primary school, or at work, are covered by regular health inspection and treatment/referral services. It should be possible to arrange for some health Screening at NFE centers of child labour.

(i) *Nutrition* : Department of Women and Child Development, Ministry of HRD, Government of India has an on going progranmme for Women and Children, i.e. Integrated Child Development Services which are approved on the basis of proposals by the State Governments and Non-Governmental Organisations. While it will not be possible to earmark funds specially for child labour, proposals from State Governments/Non-governmental Organisations and Voluntary Agencies in child labour areas will be founded on a priority basis and if, necessary, the rules could be relaxed to consider proposal from the organization be set-up for taking up welfare measures for child labour also.

(j) *Anti-Poverty Programms Coverage*: IRDPINREP/ RLEGP, etc. funds meant for poverty-alleviation programmes on the basis of criteria which have been laid down for the State to follow included in the coverage of the entire gamut of anti-poverty programme are families which have child labour and to the extent that such families with incidence of child labour fall within the selection criteria for endowment of income generating assets (i.e. IRDP) or for wage employment (NREP/RLEGP), they would be benefited by the on going programmes which have a large corpuses of funds allocated to them in 7th Plan. To the extent, therefore that the poorest families after often forced to put their children to work for wage/ quasi-wage employment, they would be getting assistance or raise themselves above the poverty lines and this, in conjunction with the Non-Formal Education Centers being opened in rural areas, slum areas, etc. will go a long way towards one of the basic causes of children being put to work, i.e. poverty.

To sum up, it is revealed from the foregoing chapter that many labour welfare legislations have been enacted from time to time to promote and improve the working conditions of child labour. Even after independence, numerous welfare legislations have been enacted by the Center and State Governments, in the light of the philosophy, contained in Indian Constitution. Besides these legislative enactments, the Governments has also adopted a *National Policy on Child Labour* in 1974. The policy resolution has evolved guidelines in the field of education, health, nutrition, integrated child development, etc. Both the Governments, i.e. Center and State are expected to carry out the guidelines of National policy to ensure the improvement of the working conditions of the child workers. It is also revealed that the child labour welfare legislation in India has been influenced to a great extent by the Conventions and Recommendations adopted by International Labour Organisation from time to time. Besides Constitutional provisions, there are at present thirteen major enactments which provide legal protection to our children in various occupations. A part from this, a recent Bill namely *"The Children's Code Bill 2000"* prepared by an expert committee under the chairmanship of justice V.R. Krishna Iyer, also deals about abolition of child labour in India in future.

3.2.2.3 More Districts Under Child Labour Elimination Project

Fifty more districts will be brought under the purview of the National Child Labour Projects (NCLP) being implemented in 13 States for the elimination of child labour. The Labour Ministry, Govt. of India runs these projects in 100 child labour endemic districts in the Country.

The Planning Commission in the Tenth Plan gave the approval for the inclusion of 50 districts having high concentration of child labour. The Planning Commission has also increased the annual budget for the projects to Rs. 602 crore in the Tenth Plan.

The NCLPs were launched for the first time in 1988 in the areas of high concentration of child labour. These are area specific and time-bound projects where priority is being given to the withdrawal and rehabilitation of children in hazardous employment. As of now, projects are being implemented in

Andhra Pradesh (22 districts), Bihar (2), Jharkhand (16), Karnataka (5), Madhya Pradesh (3), Chhattisgarh (5), Maharashtra (2), Orissa (18), Punjab (3), Tamil Nadu (9), Rajasthan (6), Uttar Pradesh (11), and West Bengal (8). So far 2.11 Million children have been covered under the projects of whom 1.87 lakh have been brought into the formal education system through special schools.

The ILO funds several International Programmes including some in India, for elimination of child labour. Five districts each in Madhya Pradesh, Uttar Pradesh and Tamil Nadu are covered under the project that have seen the enrolment of 20,000 children for elementary education, 40,000 directly rehabilitated 20,000 adolescents imparted Vocational Training and 10,000 families provided with additional income generating opportunities.

The International Programme on Elimination of Child Labour in India covers children involved in gem cutting and polishing in Jaipur, those working in textile mills in Tirupur, Carpet making in Mirzapur and glass manufacturing in Ferozpur. Besides, there is special programme being funded and run by the ILO in Andhra Pradesh for eradication of the child labour.

According to the estimates of the 55th round of the National Sample Survey Organization (NSSO) Survey 1999-2000, the number of working children in the country is 10.4 million. The 1981 Census recorded the number of child labour as 13.56 million, the 1991 census recorded the number around 11.28 million, while the 2001 Census indicates the number around 10.34 million. (Census Reports, Govt. of India, 1981, 1991 and 2001).

3.3 REFORMS HELPING IN POVERTY REDUCTION

A study by the U.N. Conference on Trade and Development (UNCATED) team in India has revealed that Maharashtra, Tamil Nadu, Gujarat, Karnataka, Andhra Pradesh and Punjab are better integrated into the global process evidenced from their growing share in the country's total exports. They have also witnessd the highest reduction in poverty rates both urban and rural. In the case of agriculture, domestic reforms would have a greater impact on rural poverty than external sector reforms even as a rise in world trade would substantially reduce the incidence of poverty globally.

In the on-going agricultural negotiations in the WTO, the UNCATED study has stated that developing countries such as India would stand to gain immensely if agricultural protectionist and trade distorting measures in developed countries are immediately addressed.

An interesting point brought out is that country to the perception of service providing employment only for the highly skilled, nearly two-thirds of the employment in the services sector might consist of low-skilled or medium skilled people.

The study is also categorical that most of the poverty gains from trade liberalization would result from India's own reforms. Describing the advent of *G-20* coalition pre-Cancun as an important opportunity for India to follow a trade reform agenda, the study observed that it would increase trade among these countries and enhance the levels of incomes and employment and have both direct and indirect effects on poverty alleviation in India.

3.3.1 Workers' Project to be Launched

The Union Government has decided to launch a pilot project on unorganized sector workers in 50 districts in the Country. The project would cover 10 lakh workers in the first year and an additional 15 lakh in the next. The project has been launched after the Cabinet recently approved the *Un-Organised Sector Workers' Bill* which entails provision of *Pension and Medical Insurance* to unorganized sector workers. Twenty-five State Capitals will be among the areas covered under the pilot project, in addition of Faridabad, Lucknow, Patna, Nellore, Ranchi, Hazaribagh, Pune, Nagpur, and Barh.

Besides above U.S. Labour Department, the International Labour Organisation and the Indian Government have launched a $ 40 million project to combat exploitative and hazardous child labour in this country on February 15, 2004. The project has been named as 'INDUS' project, the new co-operative venture in the US Labour Department's "Largest International Technical Assistance Programme". Its goal is to eliminate child labour in 10 hazardous industries in India.

4

Judicial Efforts Towards the Problem of Child Labour

The struggle for independence was over by 15th August 1947. But the attainment of independence was not an end itself. It was only the beginning of struggle; the struggle to live as an independent nation and at the same time, establish a democracy based on the ideas and need of a new Constitution forming the basic law of the land for the realisation of these ideas was paramount. Therefore, one of the first tasks undertaken by independent India was framing of a new Constitution. Accordingly new Constitution of India was adopted by the Constituent Assembly on 26th November 1949 and it came into force on 26th January 1950. There is a difference of opinion amongst the Constitutional jurists about the nature of the Indian Constitution one view is that it is a quasi federal Constitution and contains more unitary features than federal. The other view is that it is a federal Constitution. An analysis of the whole scheme of the Constitution favours the idea of a federation with strong centralizing tendency.

The Constitution of India is written and is supreme. The provisions of the Constitution which are concerned with federal principles cannot be altered without the consent of the majority of the States. The Constitution establishes a Supreme Court to decide disputes between the union and the states, or the state *interse* and interpret finally the provisions of the Constitution. In other words, Judiciary has, in a federal policy, the final power to interpret the Constitution and guard the 'entrenched provisions' of the Constitution. The Indian Constitution-makers defined the Indian structure not with an eye on theoretical but on practical considerations in designing federalism. Under the impact of world wars, international crisis, scientific and technological progress and developments and the emergence of the ideal of social welfare state, the whole concept of federalism had been undergoing a change for sometime throughout the world. There are centralizing tendencies as evidence in every federation and whether it is in U.S.A. or in Australia strong and powerful national governments have emerged in every federation. The framers of the Indian Constitution took note of these tendencies and kept in view the practical needs of the country designed on federal structure not on the footing that it should conform to some theoretical, definite or standard pattern, but on the basis that it should be able to subserve the need of the vast and diverse country like India. The Indian Constitution, therefore, constitutes a new bold experiment in the area of federalism.

The incorporation of a formal declaration of Fundamental Rights in Part III of the Constitution is deemed to be distinguishing feature of a democratic State. These rights are prohibitions against the State. The State cannot make a law which takes away or abridges any of the rights of the citizens guaranteed in the Part III of the Constitution. If it passes such a law it may be declared unconstitutional by the courts. But mere declaration of certain fundamental rights will be of no use if there is no machinery for their enforcement. Indeed, the every existence of a right depends upon the remedy for its enforcement. Unless there is remedy there is no right, goes a famous maxim. For this purpose an independent and impartial judiciary with a power of judicial review has been established under the Constitution of India. It is the custodian of the rights of citizens. Besides, in a federal Constitution it plays another significant role of determining the limits of power of the Center and States.

In a welfare state like India the impartial judiciary is above all. Its decisions are binding not only on all citizens but the Government. It could not be fair if we fail to acknowledge the role of judiciary in safeguarding, protecting and liberating the interests of the child and child labour. Specially the apex court of the country, i.e. Supreme Court and the State High Courts of the different States are taking active participation in protecting and liberating the poor and the weakest of the weak viz. child labourers and child bonded labourers from being exploited, in various ways, besides it has helped to bring in social reform and social equality.

The founding fathers of the Indian Constitution adopted the parliamentary form of government of Westminster model. But the Indian parliament and State legislatures, unlike the English parliament, owe their origin of the Constitution and derive their powers from its provisions, and therefore working within the limitations prescribed in the Constitution. Article 50 separates judiciary from executive and legislature under the Parliamentary form of government. Strict separation between executive and legislature is quite impossible. The theory of separation of power got place in a limited sense under the Constitution. There is, thus a necessary implication that the Constitution confers on the judiciary the power of scrutiny of a law made by principal legislature to declare a law void if it is found to be in consistent with the provisions of the Constitution. Thus the Indian Constitution unlike the English Constitution, recognizes the independence of the Supreme Court, though it is circumscribed by limitation put upon by the Constitution, consequently, judicial review available in India is more or less at par with the one available in U.S.A. But in the United States, a law may also be questioned on its being unjust, arbitrary or unreasonable under the cover of the 'due process of law' clauses; in other words, the wisdom of the legislature or the policy formulated in the enactment may be subjected to security by the Supreme Court, the Indian Constitution, unlike the American Constitution, does not recognize the absolute supremacy of the Supreme Court over legislative authority in all respects as the Union parliament and State legislative are supreme in their respective jurisdiction and in that wide field there is no scope for the Indian Supreme Court to play role of the American Supreme Court.

There is no bifurcation of the Judiciary between the Federal and State Governments. The same system of courts, headed by the Supreme Court administer both the Union laws and the State laws which are applicable to the cases coming up for adjudication. This is in contrast to the American System, there are Federal Courts and State Courts. In case of any dispute relating to power arises between Central and State Governments, Judiciary plays an important role in solving this. Thus, judiciary as are of the organs of the Governments has established itself very effective to resolve the dispute between Center and State. It has got its own hierarchy and is independent from remaining organs of the government, i.e. executive and legislature. The framers of Constitution have kept separate provisions in the Constitution with respect to the functions of courts. The Supreme Court and High Courts have been conferred ample power to make rules and bye laws for regulating their internal management as well as the functionings of Subordinate Courts. Supreme Court's decision is binding on all courts in the country. Since language of the Constitution is not free from ambiguities and its meaning is likely to be interpreted differently by different authorities at different times, it is but natural that disputes might arise between the Center and its constituent units regarding their respective powers. Therefore, there must be an independent and impartial authority to decide disputes between the Center and the States or the States *inter se*. This function can only be entrusted to a judicial body. The Supreme Court under our Constitution is such an arbiter. It is the final interpreter and guardian of the Constitution. In addition to the above function of maintaining the supremacy of the Constitution, the Supreme Court is also the guardian of the Fundamental Rights of the people. Truly, the Supreme Court has been called upon to safeguard civil and minority rights and play the role of "guardian of the social revolution". It is the great tribunal, which has to draw the line between individual liberty and social control. It is also the highest and final interpreter of the general law of the country. It is the highest court of appeal in civil and criminal matters.

An independent and impartial Judiciary is said to be the first condition of liberty. It is the custodian of the rights of the citizens. In a federal Constitution, it plays another important role, it determines the limits of the powers of the Center and the units. The following provisions of the Constitution are intended to secure independence and impartiality of the Supreme Court and the High Courts:

(a) The president appoints the judges after consultation with judicial authorities. In the case of appointment of the Chief Justice of India, the President must consult such judges of the Supreme Court and High Courts as he may deem necessary. For the selection of other Judges of the Supreme Court, he must consult the Chief Justice of India. The appointment of the judges of a High Court will be made by the President after consultation with the Chief Justice of India and the Governor of the State. In the case of appointment of judge other than the Chief Justice, the Chief Justice of the High Court concerned must be consulted. Thus, in the appointment of judges, the Constitution does not give absolute discretion to the Executive.

(b) Security of tenure is guaranteed to every judge. A judge of the Supreme Court or of a High Court can be removed on the ground of proved misbehavior or incapacity. The President can remove a judge only when an address has been presented against him by each House of Parliament.

(c) Salaries of the judges have been fixed by the Constitution and cannot be varied by the legislature except during the period of proclaimed emergency.

(d) Once appointed, their privileges, rights and allowances cannot be altered to their disadvantages.

(e) The Supreme Court and the High Court have been given authority to recruit their staff and frame rules regarding condition of service.

(f) Expenditure in respect of the salaries and allowance of the judges is not put to the vote of the Legislature.

(g) The administrative expenses of the Supreme Court, including salaries, allowances, and pensions payable to its officers, are charged on the Consolidated Fund of India. Similarly, administrative expenses of the High Courts are charged on the Consolidated Fund of the State.
(h) The Constitution debars the Supreme Court Judges from pleading or appearing before any court or judicial authority in India even after retirement.
(i) No discussion shall take place in the legislature of a State or in Parliament with respect to the conduct of any judge of the Supreme Court or of a High Court in the discharges of his duties.

Thus, our Constitution has done everything possible to make the Supreme Court and the High Courts independent of the influence of the executive. An attempt is made in the Constitution to make even the subordinate judiciary independent of extraneous influences. One of the articles namely Article 237 of the Constitution makes it easy for the State government to bring about separation of the executive from the judiciary and place the magistracy which deals with criminal cases on the same footing as civil courts.

4.1 JUDICIAL REVIEW

Judicial review in India is based on the assumption that the Constitution is the supreme law of the land, and all governmental organs, which owe their origin to the Constitution and derive their powers form its provisions, must function within the framework of the Constitution, and must not do anything which is inconsistent with the provisions of the Constitution. In a federal and independent judiciary whose basic function is to act as an arbiter in a dispute arising between the Center and its constituent units under the Indian Constitution, there is a specific provision in Article 13(2) which says that the State shall not make any law which takes away or abridges the fundamental rights enshrined in the Constitution, and any way made in contravention of this provision shall, to the extent of inconsistency, be void. The inclusion of this provision appears to be due to abundant caution, as, in the absence of such a provision, the Supreme Court would still have the power to examine the Constitutionality of a law on grounds of infringement of fundamental rights. This is so because Article 124(6) enjoins a judge of the Supreme Court to faithfully abide by an oath or affirmation to uphold the Constitution. It is, therefore, the duty of the Supreme Court to protect the fundamental rights against any encroachment or infringement by the State. One of the unique features of the Constitution is that a person may approach the Supreme Court directly by appropriate proceedings for the enforcement of his fundamental rights (Article 32). Even otherwise under Article 132, the Supreme Court has an appellate jurisdiction in appeals from the High Courts in a case which involves a substantial question of law as to the interpretations of the Constitution. In addition, Article 136 confers on the Supreme Court a wide Jurisdiction in its discretion to grant special leave to appeal from any judgment, decree, determination, sentence or order in any cause or matter passed or made by any court or tribunal. Any cause or matter may include any question of law as to the interpretation of the Constitution.

Although the Fundamental Rights under the Indian Constitution bear some resemblance to the Bill of Rights under American Constitution, the deliberate rejection of the 'due process of law' clause from its incorporation in the Indian Constitution has made all the difference in the nature of judicial review as it operates in India. Early in the Gopalan case, the power of judicial review was firmly established and the limitations for its exercise were clearly enunciated. The Constitution contains express provisions for judicial review of legislation as to its conformity with the Constitutional provisions. For example, the words "procedure established by law" in Article 21 means procedure established by an enacted law otherwise valid although the procedure should not be arbitrary capricious or fanciful. Certain fundamental rights are guaranteed simultaneously with permissible reasonable restrictions which may be imposed by law on the employment of these rights for certain purpose or in public interest. The determination by the legislature of what constitutes 'reasonable' is not final. It is subject to supervision by courts. However, in evaluating such exclusive factors and forming their own conception of what is reasonable, that the social philosophy and the scale of values of the judges participating in the decision should play an important part, and the limit to their inference with legislative judgment in such cases can only be dictated by their sense of responsibility and self-restraint and the sobering reflection that the Constitution is meant not only for the people of their way of thinking but for all, and that the majority of the elected representatives have in authorizing imposition of the restriction, considered them to be reasonable. Nevertheless, the Supreme Court has laid down some broad generalisation for determining the reasonableness of restrictions, e.g. the court will apply the objective standards, the restriction should not be greater than what is required by the circumstances or there should be proximate connection between the restriction and the object sought to be achieved. In this process, the power of judicial review does not make the judiciary supreme in any sense of the word. There is ample evidence in the Constitution itself to indicate that it creates a system of checks and balance as a result of which none of the three governmental organs can usurp the functions of the other or disable the other from discharging the functions entrusted to it by the Constitution.

In India, the exercise of the power of judicial review is itself made subject to limitations which are expressly provided in the Constitution. The Supreme Court has, however also evolved certain limitations which may be called as self-imposed on its power of judicial review, such as found in res-Judicata, laches, proceedings in camera, standing, waiver, etc.

It seems to have been a common understanding that the fundamental features of the Constitution, namely, secularism, democracy and the freedom of the individual would always subsist in the welfare state. In view of the above reason, a necessary implication arises in the power of parliament that the expression "amendment of this Constitution" in Article 368 means any addition or change in any of the provisions of the Constitution within the broad contours of the preamble and the Constitution to carryout the objectives in the preamble and the Directive principles applied to fundamental rights, it would mean that while Fundamental rights, cannot be abrogated reasonable abridgements of fundamental rights can be effected in the public interest.

Although the Judges enumerated certain essential of the basic structure of the Constitution, but they also made it clear that they were only illustrative and not exhaustive. According to Sikri, C.J. the basis structure of the Constitution consists of the following features:

(a) Supremacy of the Constitution.
(b) Republication and democratic forms of the Government.
(c) Secular character of the Constitution.
(d) Separation of power between the legislature, the executive and the Judiciary.
(e) Federal character of the Constitution.

The Supreme Court has thus added the following features as basic features of the Constitution to the list of basic features laid down in the Keshavananda Bharti's Case.[1]

(a) Rule of law.
(b) Judicial Review.
(c) Democracy which implies free and fair Election. It has held that the jurisdiction of the court under Article 32, is the basic features of the Constitution.

In Minerava Mills Ltd. *v.* Union of India,[2] Supreme Court held that the following are the basic features of the Constitution:

(a) Limited power of parliament to amend the Constitution.[3]
(b) Independence of judiciary.

The doctrine of basic structure has been vehemently criticized. It has been said that the Court has not precisely defined as to what are the essential features of the basic

1. Indira Gandhi Nehru *v.* Raj Narain, AIR 1975.
2. AIR 1980 SC, 1789.
3. Shri Kr. Padma Prasad *v.* Union of India, AIR 1992 SCC 428.

structure and if this doctrine is accepted every amendment is likely to be challenged on the ground that it effects some or the other essential features of the basic structure.

It is submitted that the criticism of the doctrine of basic structure cannot be justified on the ground that it lays down a vague and uncertain test. The basic structure of the Constitution is not a vague concept. The fact that a complete list of the essential elements constituting the basic structure cannot be enumerated is no ground for denying that these do not exist.

4.1.1 PIL (Public Interest Litigation)

The timeless issue of the role of Judiciary have recently been the subject of much discussion in the developing world. The growing awareness of the need for human rights protection has focused the limelight squarely on the judiciary. Judges are increasingly finding it difficult to hide behind the doctrines of judicial self-restraint and 'passive' interpretation. Their judgments in the area of fundamental rights are scrutinized by a growing international audience interested in the need to implement social justice. The prestige and legitimacy of the judiciary is being constantly called into question as an increasing number of citizens and citizens group bring their grievance directly to the portals of the Supreme Court.

The human rights movement has in many ways made the judiciary a most dynamic and important government institution. Standing between individual citizens and the wielders of power, the judiciary has become the ultimate arbiter in the area of democratic politics. The sudden thrust on to the center stage has made judging a difficult and complex exercise, especially, in the developing world. The Court often finds that it has moral responsibility without the necessary safeguards of institution at integrity. Nevertheless, a growing number of judges are gradually beginning to realize that there is really no escape from the increasing responsibility and that the time may be ripen to develop a fresh, innovative and principled approach to the role that the judiciary can play in a changing society.

One important aspect of the methodology of judging, which tests the creativity of Supreme Court judges is in the formulation of Constitutional remedies which effectively meet the issue of controversy before the court. It is this aspect in the final result which will determine whether a strong judgment of the court is empty rhetoric. Increasingly Constitutional remedies are constructed in terms of on-going judicial review as to whether the State is implementing the decision of the court. In the United States this has resulted in large scale i.e., judicial intervention in the disagregation policies of State schools. As one of Judiciary's special roles is to ensure the effective implementation of government policy in the case of individual citizens, the necessary corollary is that it devices the mechanisms to ensure that such implementation is taking place. And yet, the mechanisms should not result in the judiciary acquiring a corrective executive role.

The task in these sensitive cases is to devise mechanisms which will aim at a consensus and protect minorities without violating majority role. The courts should avoid partisanship and attempt to formulate remedies which have the support of all parties. This would of course require them to go beyond the general judicial remedies of damages and punishment. To be creative in this regard is therefore the fundamental challenge.

On the other hand, for flagrant situations of injustice, remedies presented by the courts would of course have to be different. They would not aim at a consensus but attempt to ensure effective implementation of government policy. In such a context, the judiciary must define effective mechanisms which will ensure government compliance and implementation having meaningful impact on the lives of those who have brought their grievances before the courts.

Public interest litigation is not the nature of adversary litigation. The purpose of PIL is to promote the public interest which, mandates that violation of legal or Constitutional rights of a large number of persons, poor, down-trodden, ignorant socially or economically disadvantage should not go underdressed. The Court can take congnizance in PIL when there are complains which shock the judicial conscience. PIL is *probono publico* and should not be used for any ulterior motive and no person has a right to achieve any ulterior purpose through such litigation.

Thus it is the solemn duty of the Court to protect the society from the so-called protectors of the society and, thus, while entertaining PIL, the Court should be conscious and try to ascertain the bonafides of the petitioner and further, find out whether he is really a public spirited person or he has approached the court to settle his ulterior score through the legal process.

It is settled law that a person approaches the Court of equity in exercise of it is extraordinary jurisdiction under Article 226 of the Constitution of India, he should approach the Court not only with clean hands but with clean mind, clean heart and with clean objectives.

[*Vide Ramjos Foundation* v. *Union of India, AIR 1993 SC, 852 (1992 AIR SCW 3460), G. Narain Swami Reddy* v. *Government of Karnataka, AIR 1994, SC 1726: (1991 AIR SCW 1755) and K.R. Swiniwas* v. *R.M. Premchand, 1994 (6) SCC, 620.*

The courts must do justice by promotion of good faith and prevent the law from craftly evasions. Courts must maintain the social balance by interfering where necessary for the sake of justice and refuse to interfere where it is against the social interest and public good. [vide State of Maharastra v. *Prabhu, 1994 (2) SCC 481 and Andhra State Financial Corporation* v. *Gar Re: Rolling Mills 1994 (2) SCC 647: AIR 1994 SC 2151*].

No litigant has a right to unlimited drought on the court's time and public money in order to get his affairs settled in the manner as he wishes. Every access to justice should not be misused as a license to file misconceived and frivolous petitions [*Dr. B.K. Subbarao* v. *Mr. K. Prasaran, 1996 (7) JT 265: 1996 Cri L.J. 3983, Rajesh Rathi* v. *State of Rajasthan, 1998 Cr. L.J. 1524 (Raj)*].

The present position as emerges from a consideration of cases after 1982 is that a uniform rule of standing is applied for all remedies and the rule is whether the applicant has sufficient interest. The question of what is a 'sufficient interest' in the matter of which the application relates appears to be mixed question of fact and law. It is a question of fact and degree and is the relationship between the applicant and the matter to which the application relates, having regard to all the circumstances of the case. The *locus-standi* requirement today is that any body may apply, for example, a member of the public who has been inconvenienced, or a particular grievance of his own. If the application is made by a stranger (third party), the remedy is purely discretionary. Where, however, it is made by person who has a particular grievance of his own, whether as a party otherwise, then the remedy lies *ex debito justitiae*.

4.1.2 Labour Jurisprudence and PIL

In Fertilizer Corporation Kamgar Union v. *Union of India (AIR 1981 SC 344)*, a Constitutional Bench of the court recognized the 'locus-standi' of worker to challenge the legality of sale of certain plants of Sindri Fertilizer Factory. The Court established the principle that decision taken by the management affecting their rights directly, the workers of a factory have the *'locus-standi'* to challenge major decision of management.

In *P.U.R* v. *Union of India (AIR 1982 SC 1473)*, the Court treated a letter written by petitioner organization as public interest litigation. The Court declared that right to minimum wages is a fundamental right of workers under Article 21 of the Constitution.

In *Bandhua Mukti Morcha* v. *Union of India (AIR 1984 SC 802)*, the three Judges bench of the court entertained a petition filed by an organization dedicated to the cause of release of bonded labourers from Maharastra, Madhya Pradesh, Uttar Pradesh and Rajasthan working in inhuman and intolerable condition in stone quarries situated in Faridadad and some of them were bonded labourers. The Court issued a number of directions to Central and State Governments to free the bonded labourers.

In *Shiela Barse* v. *Union of India (AIR 1983 SC 378)*, the Court issued the direction to lockup female prisoners only in female lockups guarded by female constables and to interrogate female accused only in the presence of female officials.

In *Gaurav Jain* v. *Union of India (AIR 1990 SC 292)*, the Supreme Court took cognizance of the problem of the children born to prostitutes and constituted a committee of lawyers and social activities to look into the matter. The Court also issued number of directions for the rescue and rehabilitation of child prostitute and established Juvenile Homes for them.

In *Visahakha* v. *State of Rajasthan (AIR 1997 SCC 241)*, the Court issued number of guidelines and norms to protect and to enforce the fundamental and human rights of working women against the sexual harassment.

In *Lakshmi Kant Pandey v. Union of India (AIR 1992 SC 118)*, the Supreme Court laid down various principles and norms which should be followed in determining whether child should be allowed to be adopted by the foreign parents.

One example of innovation in recent times has been the experimentation in the Indian Supreme Court of 'open letter jurisdiction' where any individual or group with bona fide intention can by open letter activate the fundamental rights jurisdiction of the Court. In addition, the Court has made provisions for setting up of commissions to inquire into the violations of groups rights, especially with regard to social exploitation. These innovations point to the need for creativity on the part of third world legal systems to cope with the actual problems which confront it. Such innovations will infact turn out to be the important effective areas of legal change.

For the present and the near future, however, there is little prospect of the Court reverting to its traditional adjudicatory posture, where people's causes appear merely as issue, argued by lawyers and decided in the mystery and mystique of the inherited common-law-like judicial process. People now know that the Court has Constitutional power of intervention, which can be invoked to arrest their miseries arising from repression, governmental lawlessness or administrative deviance. Under-trial as well as convicted prisoners, women in protective custody in juvenile institutions, bonded and migrant labourers, unorganized labourers, untouchables and scheduled tribes, landless agricultural labourers who fall prey to faulty mechanization, women who are bought and sold, slum dwellers and pavement dwellers, kin of victims of extra judicial executions—these and many other groups—now flock to the Supreme Court seeking justice. They come with unusual problems, never before confronted so directly by the Supreme Court. They can seek now extraordinary remedies, transcending the received notions of separation of powers and the inherited distinctions between adjudication on the other. They bring too, new kind of lawyer and a novel kind of judging. They add poignant twist to the docket explosion which was previously merely a routine product of the Bar committed only to justice according to the fees. They also bring a new kind of dialogue on the judicial role in changed society. The medium through which all this has happened, and is happening in Social action litigation a distinctive by-product of the catharsis of the 1975-77 emergency. What emerged as an expiatory syndrome is now a catalytic component of a movement for judicial democracy, through innovative uses of judicial power.

A striking factor of SAL is that it is primarily judge-led and even judge-induced and it is in turn related to juristic and judicial activism, an active assertion of judicial power to avert the miseries of the masses. Although there was an almost explosive assertion that judicial population had become pronounced even before the emergency, particularly in the great decisions of *Golaknath and Kesvananda Bharati* but *Bombay Kamgar Union* v. *Abdul Bhai*, 1976 is probably the first case in which Justice V.R. Krishna Iyer sowed the seed of public interest litigation in most formidable manner. In subsequent cases e.g. *Judges transfer case, PUDR* v. *Union of India, (1984), Fertilizer Corporation Kamgar Union* v. *Union of India, (AIR 1981),* Justice Y.V. Chandrachud and P.N. Bhagwati joined the movement and clearly laid down the contors and procedural aspects and their consequences for mitigating the miseries of general person at the hands of Government. In these decisions, judges who wished parliament to have unbridled power to amend the Constitution invariably sought to justify it in the name of and for the sake of, general masses in India. They sought to mould constitutional interpretation with doctrine in surcharged people-oriented ways.

The Social Action litigation may be viewed as relatively minor exercises in class-transcendence, subject to all the frailties of struggles. Back sidings are bound to occur, but it is doubtful whether, the evolution of the Court as a people-oriented institution can be arrested subsequently. Of Course, nothing is irreversible, at least history. It would require considerable mobilization of regressive forces, to return the Court to its club-house cloistering. In fact, the SAL movement is well under way to institutionalization. Hopeful signs for the growth of the SAL-type professional competence is abound. The National Legal-Aid movement is rapidly acquiring SAL orientation and more and more High Court judges are becoming SAL-prone. The response to the administration of SAL has also been mixed. The top bureaucrats seem to resent the mini-takeover of administration through creeping Jurisdiction. Their resentment is shown indifferent compliance with the courts interim directions in many proceedings but in some cases, the tenacity of SAL petitioners and of the Bench have overborne their resistance. For those who take people's sufferings seriously, there is no rejoicing but even revolutions provide occasions of celebration. The SAL is at best an establishment revolution. Still, it nourishes hope in an otherwise darkening landscape of Indian law and jurisprudence.

4.1.3 Social Interpretation

Social Action Litigation symbolizes the politics of liberation of the rules under the Constitutionalism with their struggle against the myriad excesses of power. The Supreme Court is thereby slowly marshalling a new kind of social legitimation which neither the legislature nor the executive nor political parties can contest without appearing to justify injustice and tyranny. In this process, the litigation does not disturb the pattern of institutional comity between the Supreme Court and the executive. Rather, it appears to lend a new kind of intensity to the model of judicial statesmanship which has since Independence steadily enhanced political accommodation and Constitutional compromise in certain vital areas.

Not merely in the style and process of generation of the SAL in the contemporary Indian experience is unique rather the substance of the SAL in India is also distinctive to its contemporary condition. In essence, much of SAL focuses on exposure of repression by the agencies of the State, notably the police, prison and other custodial authorities. Close to this category are the cases which seek to ensure that authorities of the State fulfil the obligations of law under which they exist and function. In other words, much of SAL is connected with combating repression and governmental lawlessness by the apex Court is basically done under Article 32 which provides fundamental right to the petitioners for filing writ petitions and Supreme Court is under an obligation on act upon them.

These features lend a special complexity to the SAL in India. On the one hand, they impact high visibility and exalted status to the cause, on the other hand, they present some specific problems for the Court. Since all the complaints on governmental apathy and lawlessness raise disputed questions of fact which the Court does not as a matter of practice normally handle and also which cannot satisfactorily deal with by affidavit evidence.

As law is a social science, its growth and development is co-related with the society. It has a creative force also and specially, in modern times, law is a powerful instrument of social development. The welfare legislations correlated with new values, new thought and ·philosophy are meant for the attainment of new national objective. It is necessary that laws should breathe the welfare spirit and resolve the social problems in a more positive and helpful way. The traditional rules of interpretation are not suited to this purpose literal or grammatical interrelation of welfare legislations are bound to fail and to produce the desired results.

It was held by Supreme Court[4] that beneficial legislation must be given liberal interpretation. If a Section is capable of two constructions that construction should be preferred which furthers the policy of the Act and is more beneficial to the employees in whose interest the Act has been passed, rather than the one which would defeat the same and render the Section illusory.

In interpreting the legislation the broad social economic objective should also be kept in view. In *B. Banerji* v. *Smt. Anita Pan*[5] while interpreting the provisions of the *West Bengal Premises Tenancy Act, 1956 as amended by West Bengal Premises Tenancy (Amendment) Act, 1969*. Justice Krishna Iyer expressed the following view:

> *"Calcutta or Cochin, for the urban people of India, the shocking scarcity of a roof to rest one's tried bones in an unhappy problem of social justice that compels control of rent and eviction laws. In the case now before us, attacking the Constitutionality of the legislation, hand cuffing the landlord-proprietor's right of eviction, the law has to be tested not merely by the cold print of the Article 19(f) but also by the public concern of Article 19(5) and the Compassionate animus of Article 39 Part III and IV of*

4. Magistisasamal *v.* Pandal Bissoi, AIR 1962 SC 547.
5. AIR 1975 S.C. 1146.

> *the Constitution together constitute a complex of promises the nation has to keep and the legislation challenged before us is in partial fulfilments of the trust with the people. These observations become necessary in limine since counsel for the respondent dismissed the concept of the social justice as extraneous to an insightful understanding of the section invalidated by the High Court".*

In giving full effect to a beneficial legislation, if hardship is caused to certain individuals that may be ignored. The Court should adopt the interpretation of a statute which will obviate purposeless proliferation of litigation, without whittling down the effectiveness of protection for the parties sought to be helped by the legislation and same should be preferred to any literal, pedantic, legalistic or technically correct alternative.

Though social legislation should receive a liberal and beneficent construction from the Courts, at the same time the Courts can not overlook the fact that liberal construction must ultimately flow from the words used in the section. If the word used in section are capable of two constructions which are shown patently to assist the achievement of the object of the Act, the Court would be justified in preferring that construction of the other which may not be able to further the object of the Act. On the other hand, if the words used in the section are reasonably capable of only one construction the doctrine of liberal construction can be of no assistance. In other words, if the language is plain and unambiguous, effect must be given to it whatever may be the consequences, for in that case the words of the statute speak of the intention of the legislature.

4.2 JUDICIARY AND CHILD PROTECTION

The Supreme Court of India, as stated has been assigned an important role, as a guardian of the Constitution and protector and guarantor of Fundamental rights.

Our Constitution accords a dignified position to the judiciary. It is the greatest unifying and integrating force of our country. The Supreme Court is at the apex the well-oriented and well-regulated judicial structure of the country. It expounds and defines the true meaning of law. It is the ultimate interpreter of the Constitution*and this puts a second brake on the legislature and the executive, the first being the political check of the people themselves.[6] The Constitution puts an obligation on every organ of the State, including the judiciary, to ashlar in a new social order in which justice-social, economic, political and equality of status and opportunity prevail.[7] The final burden of interpreting these provisions is upon the courts. Courts are to contribute to law's growth without overstepping the boundaries of the system, in other words, how to reconcile tradition and convenience or the claims of stability and those of change. It is the duty of the judiciary to recognize the development of the nation and to apply established principles of the positions which the nation in its progress from time to time assumes. The Judicial organ would otherwise separate itself from the progressive life of community and act as a clog upon the legislative and executive departments rather than as an interpreter. Indian Judiciary is charged with the duty of holding the balance even, between a state or states and the union and between the state and the citizen, and sometimes between the state and the individual. It has to hold the scales even in the legal combat between the rich and the poor, the mighty and the weak without fear or favour. The role of Judiciary in India been quite significant in promoting the child welfare. Mr. Justice Suba Rao, the former Chief Justice of India, rightly remarked:

> *"Social Justice must begin with child unless tender plant in properly nourished, it has little of growing into strong and useful tree. So, first priority in the scale of social justice should be given to the welfare of children".*[8]

It is in this spirit that the apex Court has laid emphasis on the fact that the important task of social justice is to take care of child for future of the nation.

The Constitution is a document of social revolution which imposes an obligation on every instrumentality including the

6. M. Hidayatullah, Democracy in India and judicial process, Lajpartrai Memorial Lectures Series, 1965 (Bombay: Asia 1966) p. 69.
7. The Preamble of the Constitution of Inda.
8. Suba Rao, Social Justice and Law (1974), p. 110.

judiciary to transform the *status-quo ante* into a new human order in which there will be equality of status and opportunity for all including children. The judiciary has, therefore, a socio-economic destination and a creative function.

4.2.1 Child Labour and Right to Education

The abolition of the child labour is preceded by the introduction of compulsory education. Compulsory education and child labour are interlinked. Article 24 of the Constitution bars employment of children below the age of 14 years. Article 45 is supplementary of Article 24 for if the child is not to be employed below the age of 14 years he must be kept occupied in some educational institutions.[9]

The Court in a series of cases has unequivocally declared that right to receive education by the child workers in an integral part of right of personal liberty embodied in Article 21 of the Constitution.[10] These Judicial decisions clearly demonstrate that right to education is necessary for the proper flowering of man, his mind and personality. Hence the right to education is one of the facets of right to personal liberty. Further Delhi High Court in a famous case of *Anand Vardhan Chandel* v. *University of Delhi* [11] has held that education is a fundamental right and under the Constitution. The court observed that :

"The law is, therefore, now settled that the expression of life and personal liberty in Article 21 of the Constitution includes a variety of rights though they are not enumerated in Part III of the Constitution provided that they are necessary for the full development of the personality of the individual and can included in the various aspects of the liberty of the individual. The right to education is therefore, included in Article 21 of the Constitution."

This right can be denied only by means of 'procedure established by the law' as contemplated in Articled 21 of the

9. S. Roy, "Constitutional Rights of the Child in India", Social Change, Sept. 1990, Vol. 20, No. 3, p. 4.
10. M.C. Mehta *v.* State of Tamil Nadu & Others, AIR 1991 SC 417.
11. AIR 1978, Delhi, 308.

Constitution, the procedure to be fair, just and reasonable must conform a test under Articles 14, 19 and 21 of the Constitution.[12]

Similarly, the Andhra Pradesh High Court in its momentous decision in Murali Krishna Public School case[13] pronounced that:

> "Right to education to Dalits is a fundamental right and it is the mandatory duty of the State to provide adequate opportunities to advance educational interests by establishing schools".

Child labour can not be abolished unless and until the education is made compulsory. So the relation of child labour is closely related to the child education. The Court has played a parental role while directing the Central Government to persuade the workmen to send their children to nearby schools and arrange not only for the school but also provide free of charge, books and other facilities such as transportation, etc. The court also put forth the suggestion that whenever the Central Government undertakes time it should Provide that the children of the construction workers who are living at or near the project site be given facilities for schooling and this may be done either by the Central Government itself or if the Central Government entrusts the project work or any part thereof to a contractor, necessary provision to this effect may be made in the contract with the Contractor.[14]

The Court took a realistic view of the position of children and was in agreement with the prevailing conditions of Indian society. The Court agreed that so long as there was poverty and destitutions in this country, it was difficult to eradicate child labour. The court, however pleaded for the positive role to be played by the government and desired that attempt must be made to reduce, if not eliminate the incidence of child labour, because it was absolutely essential that child should be able to

12. Smt. Maneka Gandhi *v.* Union of India, AIR 1978 SC 597.
13. AIR 1968, A.P. 204.
14. Labourers working on Salal Hydro-project *v.* State of J& K, AIR 1984, SC 177 at p. 183.

receive proper education with a view a equipping itself to become useful member of the society and to play a constructive role in the socio-economic development of the country.

The Supreme Court in *M.C. Mehta* v. *State of Tamil Nadu*[15] held that the children are means under Article 45 of the Constitution to be subjected to free and compulsory education until they completed the age of 14 years. The Court has, however observed that the Directive Principles of State policy has still remained a far cry and though according to this provision all children up to the age of 14 years are supposed to be in school, economic necessity forces grown up children to seek employment.

4.2.2 Child Labour Welfare and the Philosophy of Locus-Standi

The traditional syntax of law in regard to *locus-standi* for a specific judicial redress, sought by an identifiable person or determine class or identifiable group of persons, is available only to that person or class or group of persons who has or have suffered a legal injury by reasons of violations of his or their legal right or a right legally protected, the invasion of which gives rise to actionability within the categories of law. In a private action, the litigation is bipolar, two opposite parties are locked in a confrontational controversy which pertains to the determination of the legal consequences of past events unlike the public action. The character of such litigation essentially that of vindicating private rights, proceedings being brought by the persons in whom the right personally inhere or their legally constituted representatives who are thus obviously most competent to commence the litigation.

In contrast, the strict rule of *locus-standi* applicable to private litigation is relaxed and broad rule is evolved which gives the right of *locus-standi* to any member of the public acting bonafide and having sufficient interest in instituting an action for redressal of public wrong or public injury, but who is not a mere busy body of meddlesome interloper. The dominant object of PIL is to ensure observance of the provisions of the

15. AIR 1991 SC 147.

Constitution or the law which can be best achieved to advance the cause of community or disadvantaged groups and individuals or public interest by permitting any person, having no personal gain or private motivation or any other oblique consideration but acting bonafide and having sufficient interest in maintaining an action for judicial redress for public injury to put the judicial machinery in motion like action popularis of Roman law whereby any citizen could bring such an action in respect of public delict.

Though in our country, courts have recognized a departure from the strict rule of *locus-standi* as applicable to a person in private action and broadened and liberalized the rule of standing and thereby permitted a member of the public, having no personal gain or oblique motive to approach the Court for enforcement of the Constitutional or legal rights of socially or economically disadvantaged persons who on account of their poverty or total ignorance of their fundamental rights are unable to enter the portals of the Courts for judicial redress. As yet no precise and inflexible working definition has been evolved in respect of *locus-standi* of an individual seeking judicial remedy in the field of PIL. Truly, in-defining the role of *locus-standi,* no rigid litmus test can be applied since the broad contours of PIL, are still developing apace seemingly with divergent views on several aspects of the concept of this philosophy.

The liberalization of the concept of *locus-standi* to make access to the Court easy is an example of changing attitude of the courts. It is generally seen that all the working children are from the families which are below the poverty line having no means to ventilate their grievance regarding infringement of their fundamental rights. Keeping in view the pitiable conditions of the child workers, the apex Court has shown its generosity by relaxing the concept of *locus-standi*. The Court has shown its wisdom by injecting the philosophy of public interest litigation. The judiciary is intended to vindicate and promote public interest by rendering help to those people of the society who are unable to approach the Court because of their poor-economic conditions.

This issue of *locus-standi* has arisen in number of cases before the Supreme Court. The Supreme Court has very daringly held in a case :[16]

> "Where a legal wrong or a legal injury is caused to a person or to a determinate class of persons by reason of violation of any Constitutional or legal right or any burden is imposed in contravention of any Constitutional or legal provisions or without authority of law or any such legal wrong or legal injury or illegal burden is threatened, and such person or determinate class of persons is by reason of poverty, helplessness or disability or socially or economically disadvantaged position, unable to approach the court for relief, any member of the public can maintain an application for an appropriate direction or writ or order".

Similarly Krishna Iyer, J., in *Fertilizer Corporation Kamgar Union* v. *Union of India,*[17] also stated:

> "In simple term *locus standi* must be liberalized to meet the challenge of time".

The liberalized rule of *locus standi* has further been reflected in various Supreme Court's decisions *including Ratlam Municipality Case,*[18] *K.R. Shenoy* v. *Udipi Municipality,*[19] *Ram Kumar Mishra* v. *State of Bihar*[20] *and Bandhua Mukti Morcha* v. *Union of India.*[21]

Keeping in mind the recent development of the doctrine of PIL, and the judicial exposition of the rule governing *locus-standi,* Supreme Court should revert to the facts and examine each case brought before it and determine (1) whether the petitioner has *locus-standi* to this litigation, and (2) whether this litigation will fall within the ambit and scope of PIL seeking

16. AIR 1981 SC, 344, *Ibid.*
17. AIR 1974 SC 2177.
18. AIR 1980 SC 1622.
19. AIR 1974 SC 2177.
20. AIR 1984 SC 537.
21. AIR 1984 SC 802.

declaratory as well as injunctive reliefs. Indeed, the true public interest litigation is one in which a selfless citizen having no personal motive or any kind except either, compassion for the weak and disabled or deep concern for stopping serious public injury, approaches the Court either for (i) enforcement of fundamental right of those who genuinely do not have adequate means of access to the judicial system or denied benefit of the statutory provisions incorporated in the directive principles of state policy for amelioration of their condition or (ii) preventing or annulling executive acts and omissions violative of Constitution or law resulting in substantial injury to public interest. The newly developed law and discovered jurisdiction leading to a rapid transformation of judicial activism with a far reaching change is the nature and form of the judicial process.

So it is quite clear that the Court has widely enlarged the scope of PIL relaxing and liberalizing the rule of standing by treating letters or petitions sent by any person or association complaining violation of any fundamental rights and also entertaining writ petitions filed under Article 32 of the Constitution by public spirited and policy oriented activist person or journalists or of any organization rejecting serous petitions. It has rendered many effective pronouncements and issued manifold directions of the Central and State Governments, all local and other authorities within the territory of India or under the control of the Government of India for the betterment of the public at large in many fields in conformity with the Constitutional prescriptions. The newly invented proposition of law laid down by many learned judges of Supreme Court in the arena of PIL, irrefutably and manifestly establish that our dynamic activism in the field of PIL is by no means less than those of other activist judicial system in other part of the world. Recently in *Jantadal* v. *H. Choudhury,*[22] it has been held that Supreme Court in defining the rule of *locus-standi* has not applied any rigid litmus test as the law is still developing. In addition to above, some PIL cases decided by various High Courts and Supreme Courts where the traditional

22. AIR 1993.

rule *locus-standi* has been relaxed are namely *B.L. Wadhera* v. *Union of India*.[23] *B.L. Wadhera* v. *Union of India*,[24] *B.L. Wadhera* v. *Union of India*,[25] *B.L. Wadhera* v. *Union of India*,[26] *B.L. Wadhera* v. *Union of India*.[27]

As regards to the welfare of child labour the Court opined that Compulsory Insurance Scheme should be provided for both adult and child employees taking into consideration the hazardous nature of employment.[28]

4.2.3 Prohibition of Traffic in Human Beings and Forced Labour

As regard the true Scope and meaning of traffic in human beings and other forms of forced labour, the Court has specifically pointed out that Article 23 of the Constitution has been intended to protect the individual not only against the State but also against other private citizens. It prohibits traffic in human beings and begar and other similar forms of forced labour practiced by anyone else.

In *Lakshimi Kant* v. *Union of India*[29] the court took active steps to abolish bonded domestic service and slavery of poor children which had been in practice. But violation of various protective provision have been pertinently pointed out by the highest judicial tribunal in the country. For such violations related to the provisions of the *Minimum Wages Act, 1948, and the Inter-State Migrant Workmen (Regulation of Employment and conditions of Service) Act, 1979*, the Supreme Court has issued directions to safeguards the interests of large number of child workers in *Salal Hydro Project* v. *Jammu & Kashmir*.[30]

Despite judicial activism, there are still many cases where the vicious poverty has compelled the parents to sell their children hoping that the children would be engaged only in household duties. But there are persons, who purchase female

23. HC CWP 1796/1999.
24. HC CWP 266/2000.
25. HC CWP 3774/2001.
26. AIR 2002(2) SC 350 Para 75.
27. HC (Ranchi) WPC (PIL) No. 3482/2002.
28. AIR 1991 SC 419.
29. AIR 1984 SC 469.
30. AIR 1987 SC 177.

children for the purpose of forcing them to brothel keepers, they are brutally treated, until they succumb to the desire of the brothel keepers and enter into the unethical and squalid business of prostitution. Some of such were brought to the notice of the Supreme Court in *Vishal Jeet* v. *Union of India*.[31] The Supreme Court referred to Article 23 of the Constitution which prohibits traffic in human beings and clause (e) of Article 39, which *inter-alia*, provides that the tender age of children is not abused and the citizens are not forced by economic necessity to enter into work unsuited to their age or strength. The Supreme Court also referred to clause (f) of Article 39, which *inter-alia* provides that childhood and youth are protected against exploitation and against moral and mental abandonment. These provisions show that the framers of the Constitution were anxious to protect and safeguard the welfare of children.

It may therefore be summed up here that judiciary has always worked hard to discourage the practice of traffic in human beings and forced labour. The Courts in India are always quite sensitive to the problems of child workers who are oftenly made victim by their mighty employers. The judiciary has always fought for the cause of child workers with a zeal to raise them to higher level of achievement and bring about their total advancement and welfare so that they are converted into good citizen of the country.

4.2.4 Child Labour Welfare and Judicial Activism

The judiciary has almost brought a revolution in the life of child workers in India. It has always endeavored to expand and develop the law so as to respond to the hope and aspirations of people who are looking to the judiciary to give life and content to law. The judicial institutions in India have played a significant role only for resolving inter-disputes but also to act as a balancing mechanism between the conflicting pulls and pressure in the society. It has virtually played a vital role in the task of providing political, social and economic justice to the poor child workers in this country. No efforts seem to have been spared by the Indian judiciary to uphold the cause of the poor workers. The Courts have always interpreted and applied the

31. AIR 1990 SC 1412.

law as to promote the cause of justice and to meet the hope and aspiration of the children as per the mandates of the Constitution. The concern of the courts for the under privileged poor section of the society is aptly reflected in *Bihar Legal Support* v. *The Chief Justice of India and others.*[32]

Thus the foregoing paragraphs disclose that judiciary has always given a lead to save the child workers from exploitation and improve their working conditions. Judicial mandate clearly demonstrate that right to education is necessary for the proper flowering of children.

Further the judiciary has shown a generosity towards poor child workers by relaxing the rules of *locus-standi*. It has always made efforts to benefit the poor child workers by entertaining their problem and giving relief to them despite the limitations of *locus standi*. The observations made by the judiciary in various decided cases show that it is always committed to the causes of the child workers. The judiciary has always made concrete efforts to safeguard them against the exploitative tendencies of their employers by regularizing their working hours, fixing their wages, laying down rules about their health and medical facilities. The judiciary has even directed the States that it is their duty to create an environment where the child workers can have opportunities to grow and develop in a healthy manner with full dignity in consonance of the mandate of our Constitution.

4.2.5 The Problem of Child Labour and Judicial Response

Judiciary has been active to the welfare and protection of child labour. The role of judiciary in solving the problems of child labour is evident from following case laws decided by Supreme Court from time to time:

1. *People's Union for Democratic Rights and Others*
   v.
   Union of India and others[33]

32. AIR 1987 SC 38.
33. AIR 1952 SC 1473.

This writ petition was brought in the form of public interest litigation to ensure observance of the provisions of various labour laws, in relation to workmen employed in the construction work of different projects relating to Asian Games. The matter was brought to the knowledge of the Court by an organization formed for the purpose of protecting democratic rights by means of a letter addressed to justice Bhagwati. The letter was based on a report pepared by a team of three social scientists, who were commissioned by the first petitioner for the purpose of investigating and inquiring into the conditions under which the workmen engaged in the different Asiad projects. Since the letter addressed by the 1st petitioner was based on the report made by three social scientists after personal investigations and study, it was treated as a writ petition on the judicial side and was issued upon it *inter alia* to the Union of India, Delhi Development Authority and Delhi Administration which were arrayed as respondents.

The Court held that Asian Games take place periodically in different of Asia and this time India is hosting the Asian Games. It is a highly prestigious undertaking and in order to accomplish it successfully according to international standards, the Government of India has to embark upon various construction projects. This construction work was framed out by the Government of India among various authorities, such as the Delhi Administration, the Delhi Development Authority and the New Delhi Municipal Committee. The writ was filed to endure that the labour laws are implemented and the rights of the workers under the labour laws are not violated. These various authorities to whom the execution of the different projects was entrusted engaged contractors for the purpose of carrying out the construction work of the projects and they were registered as principal employers under Sec. 7 of the *Contract Labour (Regulation and Abolition) Act, 1970*. The contractors started the construction work of the project and for the purpose of carrying out the construction work they engaged workers through the Union of India. Clearly admitted in its affidavit in reply that the Jamadars were deducting rupee one per day per worker from the wage payble to the workers and as a result the workers did not get the minimum wage of Rs. 9.25 per day and there was violation of the provision of the *Minimum Wages Act, 1948*.

So far as the *Employment of Children Act, 1938,* is concerned the plea of the Union of India, the Delhi Administration and the Delhi Development Authority was that no complaint in regard to the violation of the provisions of that Act was at any time received by them and they had doubt that there was any violation of these provisions by the contractors. It was also contended on behalf of these Authorities that the *Employment of Children Act, 1938,* was not applicable in case of employment in the construction work of these projects, since construction industry is not a process specified in the Schedule and is, therefore, not within the provisions of sub-Sec. (3) of Sec. 3 of the Act. Obviously the contention urged on behalf of the respondents is well founded, because construction industry does not find a place in the Schedule to the Employment of Children Act, 1938, and the prohibition enacted in Sec. 3(3) of the Act against the employment of a child who has not completed his fourteenth year can not apply to employment in constructions industry. This is a sad and deplorable omission which, we think, must be immediately set right by every State Government by amending the Schedule so as to include construction industry in it, in exercise off the power conferred under Sec. 3A of the Employment of Children Act 1938. It is clear from the contents of Conventions No. 59 adopted by International Labour Organization and Article 24 of Indian Constitution that no child below and age of fourteenth years can be allowed to be engaged in construction work. There can, therefore be no doubt that notwithstanding the abuses of specification of Construction industry in the Schedule to the Employment of Children Act, 1938, no child below the age of 14 years can be employed in construction work and the Union of India, and also every State government must ensure that this Constitutional mandate is not violated in any part of the country. Here, of course the plea of the Union of India, the Delhi Administration and the Delhi Development Authority was that no child below the age of 14 years was at any time employed in the construction in that behalf was received by any of these authorities and hence there was no violation of the Constitutional prohibition enacted in Article 24. It was further held that the rights and benefits conferred on the workmen employed by a contractor under the *provisions of the Contract labour (Regulation and Abolition) Act, 1970 and Conditions of Service) Act, 1979* are clearly intended to ensure basic human dignity to the workmen if the workmen and deprived of any of these rights and benefits to which they are entitled under the provisions of these two pieces of social welfare legislation, that would clearly be a violation of Article 21 of the Constitution because Union of India, the Delhi Administration and the Delhi Development Authority which, as principle employers, are made statutorily responsible for securing such rights benefits to the workmen. That leaves for consideration of the complaint in regard to non-payment of minimum wages to the workmen under the Minimum Wages Act, 1948.

Thus, Supreme Court held that Delhi Administration and the Delhi Development Authority must be held to be under an obligation to ensure observance of these various labour laws by the contractors and if the provisions of any these labour laws are violated by the contractors, the petitioners vindicating the cause of the workmen are entitled of enforce this obligation against the Union of India, the Delhi Administration and the Delhi Development Authority by filing the present writ petition. The preliminary objections urged on behalf of the respondents must accordingly be rejected.

Having disposed of these preliminary objections, the judges turned *to consider whether there was any violation of the provisions of the Minimum of Wages Act, 1948, Article 24 of the Constriction, the Equal Remuneration Act, 1976*, and the *Inter-State Migrant Workmen (Regulation of Employment Conditions of Service) Act, 1979* by the contractors. The Union of India in its affidavit in reply admitted that there were certain violations committed by the contractors but hastened to add that for these violations prosecutions were initiated against the errant contractors and no violation of any of the labour laws was allowed to go unpunished.

2. *Writ petition (criminal No. 1179 of 1982, decided on March 2, 1983*
Labourers working on Salal Hydro project
v.
State of Jammu & Kashmir and Others[34]

34. 1984, 3 SCC, 538.

The issue of *Indian Express* dated August 26, 1982 carried a news item that a large number of migrant workmen from different states, including the State of Orissa, were working on the Salal Hydroelectric project in difficult conditions and they were subjected to exploitation by the contractors of whom different portions of the work were entrusted by the Central Government. The people's Union for Democratic Rights thereupon addressed a letter to Mr. Justice D.A. Desai enclosing a copy of the news report and requesting him to treat the letter as a writ petition, so that justice may be done to the poor laboureres working in the Salal Hydroelectric project. The letter was placed before a Bench of Supreme Court and it was treated as a writ petition and by an Order dated September 10, 1982, this Labour Commissioner, Orissa at New Delhi, the State of Jammu and Kashmir and the Labour Commissioner (J&K) should be shown as respondents to the writ petition and issued notice to the Union of India, the State of Orissa and the Assistant Labour Commissioner, Orissa at New Delhi to show cause against the writ petition. The Supreme Court also directed the Labour Commissioner, Jammu to visit the state of the Salal Hydro electric project and ascertain (i) Whether there are any bonded labourers employed on this project and if so, to furnish their names (ii) Whether there are any migrant workers who have come from other States (iii) What are the conditions in which the workers are living, and (iv) Whether the labour legislations enacted for their benefit are being observed and implemented pursuant to this order made by the Court. The Labour Commissioner, Jammu visited the site of the Salal Hydroelectric project and made an interim report on October 11, 1982. This was followed by a final report dated October 15, 1982.

It was pointed out in the final report of the Labour Commissioner (J&K) that some minors found to have been employed on the project site, but the explanation given was that "these minors accompany male members of their families on their own and insist on getting employed." The Supreme Court has pointed out its judgements in the *Asiad Workers'* case that construction work is a hazardous employment and, therefore, under Article 24 of the Constitution, no child below the age of 14 years can be employed in construction work. It is known fact that the problem of child labour is a difficult problem and it is purely on account of economic reasons that parents often want their children to be employed in order to be able to make both ends meet. The possibility of augmenting their meager earnings through employment of children is very often the reason why parents do not send their children to schools and there are large drop-outs from the schools. This is an economic problem and it cannot be solved merely by legislation. So long as there is poverty and destitution in this country. It will be difficult to eradicate child labour. In the socio-economic development of the country, we must concede that having regard to the prevailing socio-economic conditions, it is not possible to prohibit child labour altogether and, in fact, any such move may not be socially or economically acceptable to large messes of people. That is why Article 24 limits the prohibition against employment of child labour only to factories, mines of other hazardous employments clearly, Construction work in a hazardous and no child below the age of 14 years can, therefore, be allowed to be employed in construction work by reason of the prohibition enacted in Article 24 and this Constitutional prohibition must be enforced by the Central Government. The Central Government would be do well to persuade the workmen to send their children to a nearby school and arrange not only for the schools the fees to be paid but also provide, free of charge, books and other facilities such as transportation. It is suggested that whenever the Central Government undertakes a construction project which is likely to last for some time, the Central Government should provide that children of construction workers who are living at or near the project site should be given facilities for schooling and this may be done either by the Central Government itself or of if the Central Government entrusts the project work or any part thereof to a contractor, he should arrange for education of children.

3. *Criminal Appeal No. 300 of 1985,*
Decided on December 20, 1986
Sheela Barse

v.

Secretary, Children Aid Society and others[35]

35. 1986, 3 SCC, 596.

In this appeal by special leave the appellant who is a freelance journalist by profession and member of the Maharashtra State Legal Aid and Advice Committee, seeks to challenge the judgement of the Bombay High Court delivered on February 4, 1985 on a writ petition filed by her in the writ petition she made grievance about the working of the New Observation Home located at Mankhurd, which is maintained and managed by the Children's Aid Society registered under the Societies Registration Act, 1860 and has also been treated as a Public Trust under the *Bombay Public Trusts Act of 1950*. The society was founded on May 1, 1926. The Chief Minister of Maharashtra State in the ex-officio president of the governing council of the society. The said Society received grants from the State. It has set-up a Remand Home at Umerkhadi within Bombay area and it is now run as an Observation Home Under the provision of the *Bombay Children's Act, 1948*. The Society runs three Observation Homes one at Umerkhadi established in 1960 and the third, the new observation home also at Mankhurd. The appellant's letter of August 22, 1984 was treated as a writ petition by the High Court.

The Court held that children are the citizens of the future era. The proper bringing up of children and giving them the proper training to turn out to good citizens depends on the plans and policies of the country. In recent years the position has been well realized. In 1959, the Declaration of the Rights of the Child was adopted by the General Assembly of the United Nations and in Article 24 of *the International Covenant on Civil and Political Rights, 1966*, the importance of the child has been appropriately recognized. India as a party to these International Characters having ratified the Declaration has an obligation to implement the same in a proper way. *The Children's Act, 1938* has made elaborate provisions to cover this and if these provisions are properly translated into action and the authorities created under the Act become cognizant of their role, duties and obligation in the performance of the statutory mechanism created under the Act and they are properly motivated to meet the situations that arise in handling the problems, the situation would certainly be very much eased. The problem is such that does not brook delay. There is no unanimity of the problem also, though there may be a pattern, every individual case is likely to pose a situation very often peculiar to itself. A set pattern would not meet the situation, and yield the desired results. What is therefore, necessary to appropriately train all the functionaries under the statute, create in them the necessary bias and motivate them adequately to rise to the demand of every situation. It is clear that this is difficult job but an intricate situation requiring delicate handling with full understanding of the problem would definitely require appropriate manning of the machinery. The officers at the different levels called upon to performs statutory duties by exercising powers conferred under the statute have to be given the proper training and only when they will have all requisite capacity in them to handle the situation.

In recent years, children and their problems have been receiving attention both of the government as also of such enormous magnitude that all that has been done till now is not sufficient.

The Supreme Court deleted the observations made by High Court while giving the judgment, it was held that the appellant was not a lawyer and was not acquainted with the procedure followed in the court, so it was not necessary to make observation by Hon'ble Court. The appellant was a social worker and a freelance Journalist and she brought the matter before the High Court being genuinely aggrieved on account of non-implementation of the statute and being moved by the condition if the children in the new Observation Home.

4. *Writ petition (civil) No. 1262 of 1987*
   R. Chandra Segaram
   v.
   State of Tamil Nadu and Others
   AND
5. *Writ petition (civil) No. 13064 of 1983*
   District Beedi Worker's Union
   v.
   State of Tamil Nadu and Others

A letter petition received from the District Beedi worker's Union of Tirunelveli in the State of Tamil Nadu was treated as an application under Article 32 of the Constitution and notice was ordered initially to the state, Later to the Beedi Manufacturing Units within the state. In the letter, complaint was made about non-payment of appropriate dues for work taken, failure to implement the provisions of the labour laws, prevalence of contract labour system, etc. There is a connected petition also relating to the same subject matter with different ancillary reflects covering employment of child labour and non-implementation of the Beedi and Cigar Workers (Conditions of Employment) Act, 1966. The Supreme Court by an order dated 24 October 1989 appointed a social organization by name Society for Community Organisation Trust (SOCCO) for making appropriate investigation and furnish a report to the Court. After the Report was received and circulated, the state Government of Tamil Nadu and the manufacturer were given time to file their response by way of affidavits, considering the report and response of the State Government the Court made an order on 24 July, 1991.

The Hon'ble Court give following directions:

(a) *The Beedi and Cigar Workers (Conditions of Employment) Rules, 1968* should be strictly implemented to arrest the evil of not furnishing the books to the home workers.

(b) An establishment of the Regional Provident Fund Commissioner with full equipment for the purpose of implementation of the statute be located within the area and he should have direction to enforce the Act in all aspects. This establishment should start functioning within three months from now.

(c) *The labour laws as also the Beedi and Cigar Workers (Conditions of Employment) Act*, should be strictly enforced so that the workers get their legitimate dues and the conditions of employment improve.

(d) Tobacco manufacturing has indeed health hazardous, child labour in this trade should, therefore, be prohibited as far as possible, and employment of child labour should be stopped either immediately or in a phased manner to be directed by the State Governments but within a period not exceeding three years from now. The provisions of Child Labour Abolition Act, 1986 should be strictly implemented.

(e) Contract labour system, it is alleged, is indispensable in this trade. The Union Government is directed to look into this aspect of the matter and take its final decision, one way or the other within six months.

(f) Beedi trade is flourishing one Exploitation of labour is rampant in this trade. A Governmental labour establishment should be located in the area with full complement to answer the requirements of the matter.

(g) Since Beedi manufacturing process is carried more outside the factory then, within, so, the system of maintaining the registers as a regulating practice has become necessary. Great care should, therefore, be taken to ensure the maintenance of the register system, as the bulk of the employees out side the factories can be regulated only through the record maintained in the registers.

(h) *The Beedi Workers Welfare Cess Act, 1976 and the Beedi Workers Welfare Found Act, 1976*, which contain beneficial provisions should be implemented in the true spirit and since they are legislations of the Central Government, these should be made operational in the area.

(i) Grievance has been made that the pass books are not maintained in the names of actual workers. This should be ensured.

(j) The welfare Fund should be properly administrated and in the cse of death of a workman appropriate assistance should be extended out of the Fund quickly.

(k) In view of the health hazardous involved in the manufacturing process, every worker, including children, if employed, should be insured for minimum amount of Rs. 50,000 and the premium should be paid by the employer and the incidence should not be passed on to the workman.

The court disposed of these cases with the directions indicated above and hoped that the authorities, the employers and employees would try to implement the directions in true spirit.

4. *Writ petition (civil) No. 465 of 1986, Decided on October 31, 1990*
M.C. Mehta
v.
State of Tamil Nadu and Others[36]

This petition under Article 32 of the Constitution has been brought before the Court by way of a public interest litigation and is connected with the problem of employment of children in match factories of Sivakasi in Kamaraj District of Tamil Nadu State. On notice the State filed its return. Sivakasi has been the traditional center for manufacture of match boxes and fire works for almost the whole country and a part of its output is even exported. From the affidavit of the State it appears that as on December 31, 1985, there were 221 registered match factories in the area employing 27,388 workman of whom 2,941 were children.

It was held that the manufacturing process of matches and fire works is hazardous one, judicial notice can be taken of the fact that almost every year, notwithstanding improved techniques and special care taken, accidents including fatal occur because working conditions in the match factories are much that they involve health hazardous in normal course and apart from the special risk involved in the process of manufacturing, the adverse effect on health is a serious problem. Exposure of tender age to these hazards requires special attention.

The spirit of the Constitution perhaps is that children should not be employed in factories as childhood is the formative period and in terms of Article 45 they are meant to be subjected to free and compulsory education until they complete the age of 14 years. Children may, therefore, be employed in the process of packing should be done in area away from place of manufactures to avoid exposure to accident.

36. 1991(1) SCC 283.

It is necessary that special facilitates for improving the quality of life of children should be provided. This should require facility for education, scope for recreation as also providing opportunity for socialization. Facility for general education and also job-oriented education should be available and the school time should be so adjusted that employment is not affected.

It was also held that there is statutory requirement for providing facilities for recreation and medical attention. The State of Tamil Nadu was directed to enforce these facilities to attend the basic requirements. The State was also directed to take immediate steps to ensure provision of additional facilities on this scope. The Hon'ble Judge were of view that there should be a committee to oversee all out directions and it should consist of the District Judge of the area, the District Magistrate of Kamraj District, a public activist of the area, a representative of the employees and local labour officer. The State of Tamil Nadu was directed to deposit Rs. 3000 in the Registry of this court within four weeks for being given to Mr. Mehta for meeting his expenses of the petition.

7. *M.C. Mehta*

v.

State of Tamil Nadu and Others[37]

The appeal lies at the back of the saying that "Child is the father of Man". To enable fathering of a valiant and vibrant man, the child must be groomed well in the formative years of his life. He must receive education, acquire knowledge of men and materials and blossom in such an atmosphere that no reaching age, he is found to be a man with mission, a man who matters so far as the society is concerned.

Our constitution-makers were wise and sagacious as they had known that India of their vision would not be a reality if the children of the country are not nurtured and educated. For this, their exploitations by different profit-makers for their personal gain had to be first indicated and arrested. It is this need, which has found manifestation in Article 24, which is one of the

37. 1996 (6) SCC 756.

provisions in Part III of our Constitution on the fundamental right against exploitation. The framers were aware that this prohibition alone would not permit the child to contribute its might to the nation-building work unless it receives at least basic education. Article 45 was therefore inserted in our paramount parchment casting a duty on the state to endeavour to provide free and compulsory education to children. (It is known that this provision in Part IV of our Constitution is after the decision by a Constitutional Bench of this court in *Unni Krishnan* v. *State of A.P.* has acquired the status of fundamental right).

The Hon'ble Judge also gives opinion that extreme poverty, lack of opportunity for gainful employment and intermittency of income and low standards of living are the main reasons for the wide prevalence of child labour. Through it is possible to identify child labour in the organized sector, which forms a minuscule of the total child labour, the problems relates mainly to the unorganized sector where utmost attention needs to be paid. The problem is universal but in our case it is more crucial. Thus the Hon'ble Court disposed of the writ petition giving various directions.

Child labourers are the most unfortunate children of our country. They are unfortunate, not so much because they came from a background of deprivation not so much because they are deprived of the benefits of education or are cheated of their childhood, but because their own parents who should normally be watching their interests are often instrumental in their exploitation, may be compelled by poverty, or custom or ignorance.

People's *Union for Civil Liberties* v. *Union of India* is a public interest litigation under Article 32 of the Constitution based on the report of a Non-Governmental Organisation campaigning against child labour.

It was reported that one Rajput had procured five minor children from the state of Tamil Nadu by paying Rs. 500 to Rs. 1500 to their parents and took them to Maharashtra and forced them into bonded labour. One of them was beaten to death and remaining went missing. The trial court convicted the procurer for murder. Under the orders of the Apex Court the Maharashtra police traced three of them but the fourth, real brother of the deceased still remained untraced. Agreeing with the contentions of the counsel appearing for the petitioner that these boys were entitled to compensation the court directed the State of Maharashtra to pay sum Rs. Two lakhs to the brother of the decreased who was still untraced. Likewise the state of Tamil Nadu was directed to pay Rs. 75,000 each as compensation of the order three boys. The Court thus, upheld the claim in public law for compensation in contravention of human rights and fundamental freedoms the protection of which is guaranteed by the Constitution.

Another writ petition came to be disposed of by the apex court on 21.2.1997. The petitioner has contended that employment of children in any industry or in any hazardous industry to the mandates contained in Articles 39(e), (f) and 45 read with the preamble. The petitioner, accordingly sought issue of writ of *mandamus* detecting the government to take steps to stop employment of children in the Carpet industry in the state of Utter Pradesh, appoint a committee to investigate into their conditions of employment, and to issue such welfare directive as are appropriate for total prohibition on employment of children below 14 years and to direct the respondents to give them facilities like education, health, sanitation, nutritious food, etc.

Pursuant to the filing of this writ petition the Court appointed a committee to investigate and report on the engagement and exploitation of children below 14 years by Carpet manufactures. The committee, exploitation and the hazardous nature of child labour.

The court in a laudable exposition of the importance of child and childhood observed that "every nation developed or developing links its future with the status of the child. If children are deprived of their childhood socially, economically, physically and mentally the nation gets deprived of the potential human resources. According to the Court, the poverty is the root (cause) of child labour, and due to poverty children and youth are subjected to many visible and invisible sufferings and disabilities. However, total banishment of child labour may drive the children and mess them up into destitution and other mischievous environment, making them vagrant, hard criminals and prone to social risks. Therefore, ban of employment of children must begin from most hazardous and intolerable activities like slavery, bonded labour, trafficking, prostitution, pornography and dangerous forms of labour and like.

The Court while 'respectfully' agreeing with the directions given in *M.C. Mehta* v. *State of Tamil Nadu*[38] as feasible and inevitable reiterated the need for their speedy implementation to convene a meeting of Ministers of State Governments and their Principle Secretaries for evolving principles for progressive elimination of child labour and periodical reports to be submitted to the court.

It may be submitted that the assertion of the Court that poverty is the root cause of child labour is over simplification of a very complicated problem. While poverty may be one of the causes it is definitely not the main or the only cause. Also it could well be argued that poverty is because of child labour and child labour is not because of poverty.

Dispute as regards age of child labour procedure to be adopted.

Case : *Anant Construction Company* v. *Govt. Labour Officer and Inspector*.
(2006)9 Supreme Court Cases, 225
(Before Ruma Pal and Dr. A.R. Lakshmanan, J.J.)

In above case, the two legal issues that camp up for the consideration of the Supreme Court were whether the inspector appointed under the child Labour (Prohibition and Regulation) Act, 1986 had the power to pass an order holding that the labour employed by the appellant were the age of 14 as prescribed under the Act and whether he was competent to direct the appellant to pay compensation. The appellant was engaged in construction business. On an inspection visit to the construction site the respondent spotted three child labour being employed and issued notice to the appellant. Although the Appellant produced two birth certificates, one issued by the Sarpanch of the village Panchayat and the other by the Medical Officer, PHC Palem certifying that the child labour were above

38. 1991(1) SCC 283.

14 years of age, the inspector not being convinced of the age as certified, directed the appellant to deposit Rs. 20,000 per child with the Child Labour Rehabilitation and Welfare Fund in keeping with the decision in *M.C. Mehta* v. *State of Tamil Nadu (1996) 6 SCC 757.*

In a writ petition before the High Court the petitioner submitted that the inspector had no power/legal authority to decide the dispute regarding age of the child labour himself as he was bound to refer it for decision to the prescribed Medical authority under section 10 of the Act. The Court, however, did not agree with the contention of the appellant and dismissed the writ petition holding that the certificates produced by the appellant were unreliable. It did not interfere with the penalty ordered by the inspector.

The Supreme Court as analysis of Sections 10 and 16 of the Act, which speak about dispute as to age and procedure to be followed relating to offences, respectively, allowed the appeal. The court held that when the appellant employer produced certificates of age, the inspector was bound to refer the aatter under Section 10 of the Act to the prescribed Medical authority. He was neither competent to decide the issue nor was he entitled to hold that in the absence of certificate of age, his own survey report would stand.

The Court further held that the jurisdiction of inspector under section 16(2) to file a complaint did not extend to trying of the said complaint himself, which only courts, not inferior to the metropolitan Magistrate or a Magistrate of the first class, are competent to try. Moreover, he had no jurisdiction to impose fine, which was contrary to Section 16(3) of the Act.

The court had no hesitation in setting aside the impugned order of the inspector being without jurisdiction and also the order of the High Court upholding the order of the inspector. It is submitted that the court has rightly delineated on the powers of the inspector and the limitations thereon under the Act.

Ajay Goswami v. Union of India
(2007) 1 Supreme Court cases 143
(Before Dr. A.R. Lakshmanan and Tarun Chatterjee, J.J.)
(Writ Petition (C) No. 384 of 2005, decided on December 12, 2006)

The petitioner's grievance was that the freedom of speech and expression enjoyed by the newspaper industry was not in balance with the protection of children from harmful and disturbing materials. That though the press is free to express its ideas, at the same time, individuals also have a right to their own space and the right not to be exposed against their will to other's expressions of ideas and actions.

By way of this petition, the petitioner requested the Court to direct the authorities to strike a reasonable balance between the fundamental right of freedom of speech and expression enjoyed by the press and the duty of the Government, being signatory to the United Nations convention on the Rights of the child, 1989 and the Universal Declaration of Human Rights, to protect vulnerable minors from abuse, exploitation and harmful effects of such expression. The petitioner requested the Court to direct the authorities concerned to provide for classification or introduction of a regulatory system for facilitating climate of reciprocal tolerance which could include:

(a) An acceptance of other people's rights to express and receive certain ideas and actions; and
(b) Accepting that other people have the right not to be exposed against their will to one's expression of ideas and actions.

The reciprocal tolerance was further necessary considering the growing tendency amongst youngster and minors of indulging in X-rated jokes, SMSs and MMSs. Nudity in photographs, discussions on Sex matters, double meanings, etc. titillate and confuse young minds.

The lawyer petitioner who appeared in person submitted that he had filed this petition to seek protection from the Supreme Court to ensure that minors were not exposed to sexually exploitative Materials, whether or not the same were absence or were within the law. The real objective was that the nature and extent of the Materials having sexual content should not be exposed to minors indiscriminately and without regard to the age of the minor. The discretion in this regard should rest with the parents, guardian, teachers or experts on sex education.

The petitioner was not in any way seeking restraint on the freedom of press or any censorship prior to the publication of article or other material. The Petitioner was only seeking for regulation at the receiving end and knot at the source.

The Supreme Court in the present matter dismissed the writ petition and held that the petitioner had failed to establish his case clearly. The petitioner only stated that the new items that are published by Respondents "leave much for the thought of minors". The Court further held that fertile imagination of anybody, especially of minors should not be a matter that should be agitated in the court of law. The court also observed that the request made by the press council of India to amend some provisions should be seriously looked into by the government of India and appropriate amendments be made in Public interest.

The role of judiciary in India has quite been significant in promoting the welfare of child labour. The study discloses that judiciary has always given a leading role to save the child labourers from exploitation and improve their working conditions. Judicial decisions clearly reflect the view that right to education is necessary for the proper development of children, his mind and personality. The Court has held that education is fundamental right under our Constitution. Child labour can not be abolished unless and until the education related to the child education is enforced properly. The Supreme Court in *M.C. Mehta's case* has observed that the children in terms of Article 45 are entitled to get free and compulsory education till they complete the age of 14 years. Further the judiciary has shown a generosity towards child labour worker by liberalizing the rules of *locus-standi*. It has always made efforts and benefit the poor child worker by entertaining their problems and giving relief to them despite the limitations of *locus-standi*. Whenever a legal wrong or legal injury is caused to the child worker by their employers, the judiciary has come forward to help them by enlarging the scope of *locus-standi*. The judiciary has even directed the states that it is their duty to create an environment where the child workers can have opportunities to grow and to develop in a healthy manner with full dignity in consonance of the mandate of the Constitution of India. Consequently, the parliament in furtherance of judicial decisions, amended the Constitution and added Article 21A through *Constitution (86th) Amendment Act,* treating right to education to tender age children as a fundamental right.

5

Problem of Child Labour in West Bengal

Analytical Study of Empirical Study of Different Districts of West Bengal

5.1. OPINIONS OF EMINENT PERSONS

Child labour is a complex problem that defies simple solutions. Most recent ILO estimate indicates that an estimated 120 million children between the ages of 5 and 14 work full time in developing counties. The number rises to 250 million if secondary activities are also included.[1] Child labour is caused by a range of demand and supply factors, including others, and social and economic exploitation of poverty, the lack of access to relevant and quality education, and societal attitudes. However,

1. ILO, Child Labour, Targeting the Intolerable, Geneva, 1996.

this acute problem is being tackled by every corner of the world and India is not an exception to it. Various NGOs, social activities, welfare organizations and statesmen and trying their level best to eradicate this social problem from root level. The Government of India has also adopted long-term as well as short-term policies to face the challenge of child labour. The opinions of some eminent personalities have been collected by the researcher to ascertain the view regarding the problem of child labour.

1. *Late Shankar Dayal Sharma, Ex-President of India (Teacher's day, Sept. 5, 1994):* Neither tradition nor economic necessity can justify child labour and the major challenges in the field of education today. We can not be complacent when our primary school attendance rates has barely crossed 50% when only 40% of the children who join complete the first four years and when the total number of illiterates in the country has grown by almost 200 million since independence.
2. *Malesh (Social Activist):* 12 years old who ran away to the M.V. Foundation's Camp from rescued bonded labourers at Medipali village, near Hyderabad, India I am learning to read and write. That's something I always wanted to do—my father threatened to beat me up if I so much as said a word about going to this camp. I can never forget the thrill I felt when I came here. This is my home now.
3. *Late P.V. Narasimha Rao (when he was prime minister of India, 1995)*: Child labour is a sad reality of our world. Whenever it is practiced, it has to be eliminated. Inducing children to education is clearly to achieve this objectives.
4. *Swami Agnivesh : Bonded Labour Liberation Front,* New Delhi (1994): . . . On November 19, 250 child labourers, haling from various sectors like the silksari industry brick kilns stone quarries and glass industry, begged for an audience with the prime minister so as to present a memorandum of demands, on behalf of their 60 million brethren in servitude. It was

distressing and painful that they were not granted permission to see the Prime Minister, as the latter had no time for them . . . Gandhi has a message to the first prime minister of India . . . whenever you are in doubt, recall the face of the poorest and the most helpless man whom you have seen and asked yourself if the step you contemplate is going to be of any use if him . . . will it restore to him control over his destiny.

5. *Ramdev* : 14 year old rescued from the carpet looms of Arayee village, Allahabad the Bachpan, Bachao Andolan (save childhood movement, 1995) when I was first taken to the loom, I was promised Rs. 1000 per month and told that I would have to weave chaddars. But I was made to work on carpets and given a target of five inches per day. If the target was not completed, I was beaten up mercilessly and deprived of food. Our life was restricted to a room and we even were given only just bags to sleep on. We defecated inside the same room.
6. *P.A., Sangama : M.P. (when he was minister for Labour, 1995):* Exploitative child labour whenever it is practiced is a moral outrage and an affront to human dignity.
7. *Late Madhav Rao Scindhia* : M.P. and former minister for Human Resources Development (When he was a Lok Sabha M.P. 1983): India has the dubious distinction of having the largest child labour force in the world— 16.5 million according to ILO statistics— three years have passed since the International Year of the child celebrated. Despite pious declaration nothing really has taken place in India. The various laws dealing with child labour should be consolidated into one comprehensive code with uniform definition. Loopholes in the existing law must be plug and there must be stringent penal provisions for violating the law. The number of inspectors must be increased and the erring once should be punished. There must be compulsory informal education, compulsory health checks and improvement in working conditions. An

increase in the minimum wage for children can be contemplated because economic necessity drives them to work. If we can increase the minimum wage for children and restrict their hours of work, parents will still get the same amount of income. Children must grow as the brightest flowers in the country's garden. Let them not decay and fade away.

8. *Chitra Naik : Member, Planning Commission, New Delhi, (1994, and 1996):* The issue of universalisation of education in general and education of girls in particular was raised by eminent persons several decades ago. Jyotiba Phule raised the issue of universal primary education in 1882. Gokhale presented his will in 1910 and Karve established the Women's University in 1916, the irony is that the same set of questions and issues are being raised even today. The universalisation of education is so important in the present context that it needs to be addressed frontally.
9. *Anil Bordia : (When he was Education Secretary, Govt. of India, 1990):* According to statistics, the gap in education of girls and the education of boys has continued to wider over the last 30 year. Nothing new is being done as far as girls' education is concerned. That is the reason why, while the percentage of children receiving education is increasing, the increase is only marginal. If the rate of increase of population is taken into account as well, the educational gains are more or less neutralized and the number of girls who have had no education is, in fact increasing very dramatically.
10. *Anjana Mangalagiri : UNICEF field office, Bhubaneswar (1994):* It is not enough to enrol more girls as students and women as teachers if the content of that education remains unchanged (or if barriers to girls) participations in education as a result of their subordination are not removed. It is thus imperative that the process of educational planning assumes sensitivity to the strategic gender needs.

11. *Joseph Gathia* : Director, Center of Concern for Child Labour, New Delhi (1995): In fact, way back in 1989 several NGOs including the center of concern for child labour pressed for a four-point action agenda at the U.N. subcommittee on the contemporary forms of salvery in Geneva. We stressed that to tackle the phenomenal growth in the number of children entering the labour market in the developing countries one of the effective measures is to focus on primary education.... the crux of the problem lies not merely in introducing primary education but in the quality of education.
12. *Rita Panicker, Butterflies an NGOs, New Delhi, (1994):* child labour in India is legal, except in the hazardous industries listed in the Child Labour (Prohibition and Regulation) Act. By presenting these children from earning a fair day's wage, the elite forces children into illegal activities like drug-peddling, Liquor vending, prostitution, begging and pick-pocketing.
13. *Amod Kanth,* Senior police officer and founder of Prayas an NGO (1994): These children work for their living and are exploited by everyone—their parents, employers and the municipal authorities. The police have a wrong attitude towards these children and often arrest child hawkers and boot polish boys when there is no such thing as 'arrest' under the Juvenile Justice Act. The police don't understand that a different role is required from them under this Act.
14. *Syed Muitoba Hossain, student editor, Human Rights Forum National Law School of India University, Bangalore (1995)*: All these initiatives which the Government has undertaken seem to be quite laudable, but it is their implementation that posses a problem. What is lackling is in fact the political will to implement these programs. Moreover, there is—(no) authentic data-base. The compilation of relevant data on the basis of the 1991 census is getting unduly delayed. The suggestion of the parliamentary standing committee for instituting comprehensive, time bound, socio-

economic study state-wise in identified areas of the child labour concentrations deserves to be taken most seriously—otherwise this basic infirmity will vitiate the planning process and erode the credibility of the claims of 'achievement'.

15. *A view from the Indian Ministry of Labour, Govt. of India:* The exploitation of child labour, particularly in hazardous occupations and dangerous operations, is an unethical practice and an illegal one too. A crime indulged in by the poor parents who send them to employment for a few rupees more. And perpetuated by the employers who exploit cheap labour, extracting 14-16 hours of work in a day—almost twice the prescribed hours of work.
    But isn't it time, we spared a thought to at least those small children who are employed in hazardous occupations and dangerous operations? Isn't it time they too get educated? Isn't it time, they enjoyed their childhood? Isn't time, they too were given a change to grow big. LET US ALL TRY TO PUT THEM IN SCHOOL (*Source*: excerpted from MOL advertisement, National dailies 30th July 1995).
16. *Justice P.N. Bhagwati, Former Chief Justice of India,* "The child is a soul with a being, a nature and capacities of its own, who must be helped to fine them, to grow into their maturity, into a fullness of physical and vital energy and the utmost breath, depth and height of its emotional, intellectual and spiritual being otherwise there cannot be a healthy growth of the nation".
17. *V.R. Krishna Iyer, Former Judge, Supreme Court of India,* "The blood and tears, sweat and toil of young innocents are an integral part of India's foreign exchange earning. Hardly a single case and the implementations of child protection legislation is the waterloo of welfare jurisprudence relating to the most vulnerable of this human sector".
18. *A.P. Verma,* Director, National Labour Institute: "Children are an assets for any society. It is the responsibility of society to nurture them through

various phases of their development to enable them to make to meaningful contribution of the society".

19. *Pushpendra, Consultant CDS, LBSNAA, Mussorie* : "The paradox, however, remains. Notwithstanding half a century of independence, a large section of the intelligensia and officials continue to blame our colonial past for the problems we face today, and yet the policies and practice of the colonial regime continue unabated! Regrettably this paradox is widely accepted but has seldom been seen a problematique".

20. *Dr. Mahaveer Jain, fellow of the V.V. Giri National Labour Institute, Noida:* "Few abuses of human rights are so universally condemned, but at the same time so universally practiced as child labour. By any objective measure this issue should rank high on the global agenda, but, in practice, it is surrounded by a wall of silence and perpetuated by ignorance. Child labour continues to be and affront to the consequence of the world community. Today we have an opportunity and duty to bring this evil practice to an end".

21. *Shantha Sinha, Secretary trustee of the M. Venkatrangaiya Foundation, 98, Marredpapally, West Secundrabad, 500096:* "All non-school going children are child workers in one from the other. Agriculture child labour constitutes the core of the problem. Child labour policies and education policies have to be formulated and operated in tandem. Parents do not send their children to get educated and poverty as a limiting factor is highly over-rated. Motivation and availability of infrastructure rather than poverty are the key factors. The paper underlines the strength of formal education in eradicating child labour forcefully argues for legislation to provide for compulsory education".

22. *Dr. Sayyasachi, Lecturer, Department of Sociology, Jamia Milla Islamia, Jamia Nagar, New Delhi-110025* : "Modernity generates several pathologies of which child labour is one destroy children and childhood. They undermine processes of building up social and human capital for development, their structure is

linked to such social and cultural values that support the modern industrial production system. The violence that is generated from this system creates child labour".

23. *Amarjeet Sinha, Dy. Director, LBS National Academy of Administraion, Mussoie"*: "The Indian child is a victim of widespread poverty and insufficient publication. The inability to provide free and compulsory education to every child is the most serious failure of our democratic experiment. On the one hand poverty alleviation has to be strengthened, to do away with child labour. On the other hand, it should be stressed that poverty in a nation does not come in the way of public action to make primary education compulsory. Improving school education, creating adequate space for community participation and promoting development of shills within the precincts of school at an early age can all play an important role in motivating poor parents to send their children to school.
24. *Rudi a Belgain Scholar* : "The PEOBLEMM WOULD NOT GO *away all by itself.* Even if there are areas where child labour seems to be disappearing, there are as many and more where child labour is just starting to make its appearance".
25. *Human Folks, The Chairman of the United States National Child Labour Committee*: "—Any work by children that interfere with their full physical development, their opportunities for a desirable minimum of education on their needed recreation".
26. *Prof. Smt. N. Acharji, Xavier Labour Research Institute, Jamshedpur* : "Books and stationary are expensive. Will the parents choose between food and clothing, the primary needs or purchase books for the children? For scheduled caste and tribes even these may be available free of cost. But all poor families the question posed is immediate supplementary income and to use the children as sources rather than postpone this prospect to an uncertain date, when he will pass his matric and may or may be not get a job

in an economy when millions are still unemployed. Thus psychologically the path of least resistance is adopted by them.

27. *M.P. Joseph & Goutham Banerjee—National Program Co-ordinator, IPEC of ILO in India, formerly Labour Commissioner, Government of Kerala and Advocate, Supreme Court of India*: "Many trade unions may not have yet fully understood the concerns of damage they are doing to themselves and their workers by permitting child labour to continue".
28. *Meena Gupta, Project Co-ordinator, CLASP, ILO:* "Inspite of laws child labour continues to exist in prohibited industries and areas of employment, and is subject to very little regulation and control in non-prohibited industries and areas of employment". "Attitudes among parents equally contribute to the non-enforcement of child labour laws and regulations". "Since birth certificates are not common in the rural area among poorer people in India, there is no reliable evidence to prove the age of the child". "In the absence of a compulsory education law of children in India, parents are under no legal compulsion to send their children to school".
29. *Late V.V. Giri: The term "child labour" is commonly interpreted in two different ways:* First, as social evil. In the first context it signifies employment of chidden in gainful occupation with a view to adding to the labour income of the family. It is in the second context the term child labour is now more generally used. In assessing the nature and extent of the social evils, it is necessary to take into account the character of the jobs in which the children are engaged the danger to which they are exposed and the opportunities of development which they have been denied.

Thus the opinion expressed by eminent personalities create awareness among common people with regards to eradication of child labour. Seminar, workshop, symposium, etc. can also render great assistance to arrest this evil practice.

5.2 EARLIAR SURVEYS

The global awareness on child labour has evolved during this century including India. There are several important international instruments on child labour, the most important are the ILO's Minimum Age Convention No. 138 and the UN Conventions on the Rights of the child. According to the 1991 census estimates, around 11.28 million children between the age of 5 and 14 are engaged in child labour and 10 million children in this age group.[2] However, other estimates of child labour in India range from some 40 million to over 100 million child workers engaged primarily in agriculture and allied activities in rural areas and in a variety of industries including informal sector activities in the urban areas. The most exploitative forms of child labour include child prostitution, forced and bonded labour which is found in some part of the country. The situation of the girl child labour in the country would call for particular attention.

TABLE 5(2).I.
Distribution of Child Labour in the World

	No. (M)	*% Share in the total*
South East Asia	29.0	55.77
Remaining Asia	9.1	17.5
Africa	9.7	18.65
South (Latin) America	3.1	5.96
Europe	0.7	1.34
North America	0.3	0.57
Oceania	0.1	0.19
World (Total)	52.0	100.00

Source : International Labour Organisation, (noted from) "Award Digest", Vol. XX, No. 7-12, July-Dec. 1994, p. 1.

2. Chaudhuri, A Dynamic Profile of Child Labour in India, 1951-91, ILO, New Delhi, 1996.

TABLE 5(2).2
Child Workers in Selected Countries

Country (Year)	*Age Group*	*% of economic activity in age group*
Africa		
Bostwna (1984-85)	14-Dec.	12.7
Burkina Faso (1985)	—	69.2
Burundi (1986)	Under 14	15.8
Egypt (1984)	Under 14	8.2
Malawi (1987)	—	52.7
Nigeria (1986)	—	3.3
Senegal (1988)	19-Oct.	32.5
America		
Argentina (1989)	—	6.6
Bolivia (1989)	19-Oct.	19.3
Brazil (1989)	—	18.8
Costa Rica	14-Dec.	13.5
Ecuador (1989)	—	8.5
Gautemala (1986-87)	—	18.3
Haiti (1988)	—	24.0
Maxico (1988)	—	11.5
Paraguay (1989)	—	24.0
Haiti (1988)	14-Dec.	22.5
Peru (1989)		2.8
Asia		
Bangladesh (1985-86)	—	19.5
India (1981)	Under 14	5.2
Indonesia (1989-90)	—	12.4
Sri Lanka (1985-86)	—	16.6
Syna (1984-86)	—	4.9
Thailand (1984)	—	5.2
	14-Nov.	20.9
Europe		
Greece (1987)	—	1.3
Portugal (1987)	—	6.7
Turkey (1988)	14-Dec.	27.3

Source : ILO Year Book of Labour Statistic 1998-89 and 1989-90, 'Award Digest', *Journal of Labour Legislation*, (Vol. XX, Nos. 7-12, p. 2).

According to an estimate of ILO (1985), there were 62 million child labour in the world. The South-East Asian Countries accounted for 55.77% followed by the remaining Asian countries (17.50%), Africa (19%) and South America (6%) [see Tables 5(2)1 and 5(2)2]. As regards India, various unofficial estimates place the number of child labour between 44 million and 100 million. Census reports and National Sample Surveys data are two major official sources of statistics on the incidents of child labour in India.

According to the census reports of 1971, the total number of child labour in India was 10.74 million. By 1981 was 13.6 million and by 1991 it was 16.8 million. But by 2001, it has been reduced to 14.7 million. As per the census 1991, nearly 86 percent were working in the agriculture sector and the rest in the other sectors. According to a study of the Labour Bureau Shimla (1996), employment of child labour in factories was almost a negligible 0.7% of the total average daily employment. The unorganized sector and informal sector, both in the urban and the rural areas accounts for almost all the child labour force. According to National Sample Survey (47th Round) there were 18.33 million child labour in 1992-93 and 1976 million in 2003 (49th Round). Approximate 90% of child labour were in the rural area [Table (5(2).3] Child Labour Constitutes 5.2 percent of the total labour force in comparatively much less than the proportion in large number of African, South-East Asia and the remaining Asian countries. However, in aggregate terms, India has the largest population of child labour.

This distribution of child labour in various states appears to indicate certain correlations. States having a larger population living below the poverty line have a higher incidents of child labour. Similarly, the higher effective rate of enrolment in schools at the primary level and lower rate of dropouts are accompanied simultaneously by lower incidents of child labour. Conversely the lower effective rate of enrolment of children in schools at the primary level and a higher drop-out rate are accompanied by higher incidence of child labour. States having a higher literacy rates are found to have lower incidence of child labour while lower literacy rates accompanied by a higher incidence in that states having large number of agricultural labour have higher incidence of child labour and *vice versa* [see

TABLE 5(2).3
Activity-wise Distribution of Child Workers in the Year 2001

Sl. No.	Name of activity	Total No. of child workers	% of child workers to total
1.	Cultivations	3,999,769	35.73
2.	Agricultural labourness	4,787,548	42.75
3.	Livestock, orcheds, etc.	716,4278	6.40
4.	Mining and quarrying	23523	0.21
5.	Manufacturing and processing, servicing and repairs, etc.		
	(a) Household Industry	432.983	3.87
	(b) Other than household industry	544,291	4.86
6.	Construction	85,415	0.78
7.	Trade and commerce	249,205	2.23
8.	Transport storage and communication	35,547	0.32
9.	Other Services	320,826	2.85
	Total Workers	11,195,535	100.00

Source : "Award Digest", *Journal of Labour Legislation*, (Vol. XX, Nos. 7-12, p. 3).

Table 5(2).4)]. Child labour is subjected to multiple forms of exploitation and is generally paid low wages. In many cases, they are piece-rate wage earners and in many occupations and areas, the minimum wages fixed for them are lower than the minimum wages for adult workers. Though various Acts provide for shorter working hours for these children but in reality working children are subjected to long hours of work. Some studies conducted by National Labour Institute have shown that the average weekly earnings of girl child labour in the match industry in the Sivakasi (Tamil Nadu) ranges from Rs. 12 to Rs. 60 per week and that a majority of them earns an average weekly wage which approximates to the lower end of the spectrum. Similarly, it was found that a child working in the

TABLE 5(2).4
Drop-out Rates 1998-99

	Class I-V			*Class I-VII*			*Class I-X (5-14 years)*		
	Boys	*Girls*	*Total*	*Boys*	*Girls*	*Total*	*Boys*	*Girls*	*Total*
(1)	(2)	(3)	(4)	(5)	(6)	(7)	(8)	(9)	(10)
All	46.74	49.69	47.93	59.38	68.31	65.40	71.68	79.46	75.36
SC	47.24	53.39	49.62	64.37	73.60	60.08	85.62	85.62	79.88
ST	61.94	68.73	64.53	76.21	81.45	78.08	84.87	84.91	86.72

SC = Schedule Caste, ST = Schedule Tribe.

Source : Ministry of Human Resource Development, Dept. of Education, Govt. Annual Report, Part -1, 1993 quoted from (Vol. XX, Nos. 7-12, p. 5), 'Award Digest' : *Journal of Labour Legislation*.

potter industry of Khurja (Uttar Predesh) gets an average monthly wage between Rs. 120 and Rs. 130. This average would be aversely affected if one pottery industry remains closed for one reason or the other such as non-functioning of kilns/ furnaces due to wet coal during the rainy season or non-availability of coal due to many reasons including transportation.

A survey carried out in 1986 by the Govt. of West Bengal regarding the prevailing conditions of child labour in different establishments such as hotels, restaurants, tea stalls, small engineering units, etc. revealed that 4.5 percent received cash wages below Rs. 50 per month, 54.74 percent between Rs. 50 and 100 and 17.89 percent received wages which ranged between Rs. 100 and Rs. 115 per month.

A child invariably works under extremely adverse conditions. The working conditions are often unhealthy and unsafe. Employment of child labour, and that too at low wages and in adverse conditions deprives them of the opportunity to develop themselves physically, emotionally and intellectually. Their productive capacities are sub-optimally developed. It can be said that employment of every child labour represents a low wages, in fact tends to depress general wage levels as well. The practice of child labour thus impose an enormous societal cost.

In India, so far, no systematic study on the earnings of under child workers has been done. In such a situation, the question of analyzing the structure of earnings of urban working children does not arise. The bulk of the urban child labour is unpaid, particularly those engaged in household activities in their homes and those supporting their parents and other family members at work sites, such as construction and mining.

Even in the formal sector, a large number of children who works as apprentices are not paid under the excuse that the employers impart free training to enable children to earn more in future. However, micro-level studies reveal that Urban working child's earning vary between zero and 200-300 rupees per month, depending on the nature of their work and sector of employment. The child workers are paid on piece-rate basis, weekly basis, contract basis and monthly basis depending on the nature of their works. Again, there exist age discriminations

TABLE 5(2).5
Estimates of Child Labour in India—1961-2000

Source	Age Group	Rural			Urban			Grand Total
		Male	Female	Total	Male	Female	Total	
(1)	(2)	(3)	(4)	(5)	(6)	(7)	(8)	(9)
Census 1961	0-14	8.16	5.56	13.72	0.58	0.23	0.81	14.53
	5-9	0.80	0.52	1.32	0.03	0.01	0.04	1.36
	10-14	7.36	5.04	12.4	0.55	0.22	0.77	13.77
	5-14	8.16	5.56	13.72	0.58	0.23	0.81	14.53
NSS (1972-73)27th (Round) (usual status)	5-9	0.88	0.63	1.51	0.05	0.03	0.08	1.59
	10-14	7.78	5.75	13.53	0.8	0.41	1.21	14.74
	5-14	8.66	6.38	15.04	0.85	0.44	1.29	16.33
NSS (1st March 1978)	5-9	0.88	0.63	1.51	0.05	0.05	0.1	1.62
	10-14	7.96	5.21	13.77	0.94	0.53	1.47	14.62
	5-14	8.84	5.84	14.68	0.99	0.99	1.57	16.25
Census 1981	0-14	7.34	5.21	12.55	0.76	0.29	1.05	13.59

(Contd.)

TABLE 5(2).5 (Contd.)

(1)	(2)	(3)	(4)	(5)	(6)	(7)	(8)	(9)
(1st March)	5-9	0.90	0.64	1.54	0.06	0.06	0.12	1.66
	10-14	8.40	5.59	14.03	1.07	0.6	1.67	15.70
	5-14	9.34	6.23	15.57	1.13	0.66	1.79	17.36
1985	5-14	—	—	—	—	—	—	17.58
1990	5-15	—	—	—	—	—	—	18.17
2000	5-14	—	—	—	—	—	—	20.25

Source : Planning Commission, Census of India 96, 97, 98*.

*Estimate for the quinquenial age-group are based on a specific study vide Appendix V of the Report of the Expert Committee on Estimates of Unemployment Planning Commission, 1970.

Projections for 1978 and 1983, 1985, 1990, 2000 based on status rates of NSS, 2nd round (1977-78). National Labour Institute. Award Digest : *Journal of Labour Legislation* (Vol. XX: 7-12, p. 42).

between adults and child workers and male and female child workers.

The problem of child labour, despite effective policies, program and legislative support, continues to persist particularly in the unorganized and home-based industries and domestic services. The populations of child workers had no doubt, come down from 13.6 million in 1981 to 11.3 million in 1991, but as per the NSS survey it has reportedly gone up to 17 million in 1997. This constitutes 3.5 per cent of the total child population. In certain industries like carpet weaving, beedi-making, match box, fire works, bangles making, etc. children are subjected to long working hours, poor working conditions, low wages and occupational hazardous which affect them adversely.

Child prostitution is an emerging problem with serious social consequences. According to a study on the problem of prostitution conducted by the *Central Social Welfare Board (CSWB) in 2001*, the estimated number of prostitutions in six metropolitan cities of Bangalore, Mumbai, Kolkata, Delhi, Hyderbad and Chennai ranged from 90,000 to 1,30,000, of this the number of child prostitutions has been estimated as 12 to 15 per cent. The religious practices of offering young girls to temples in the name of Devdasi, Basavi, Yellamma, Jogin, etc. are prevalent in certain parts of the country.

The increasing number of street children who are estimated to be 4.15 lakhs in 8 major cities of Bangalore, Mumbai, Kolkata, Delhi, Hydrabad, Indore, Kanpur and Chennai, is another serious problem. Efforts to meet the needs of street children viz. education, health, counseling, etc. through voluntary organizations have been too recent to have any appreciable impact on their status. Juvenile crimes, though declining, are still very high and the rehabilitation of juvenile delinquents vagrants requires priority attention.

India is the home of 320 million children below the age of 14 years, as per the census of 1991, which is the largest in any country of the world. Considering that opportunities of early childhood development determine the present and future human resource development of the nation, child development become a focused activity from the very First Year Plan (1952-56). In successive five year plans the country made conscious efforts in evolving and crystallizing new perspective and paradigm to initiate multillinear interventions requires to fulfil the needs of the deprived and underprivileged children. Thus the Fourth Five Year Plan (1969-74), focused an accelerating the basic minimum services for children culminating finally in the adoption of a National Policy for children in 1974, the Fifth Five Year Plan (1974-79) saw a shift in focus child welfare to child development and an emphasis on integration and coordination of service by the launching of Integrated Child Development Scheme in 1975, the Sixth Five Year Plan (1980-85) reiterated the approach and strategy outlined in the fifth plan, and promoted consolidation and expansion of the programs started earlier. The Seventh Five Year Plan (1985-90) led to spatial expansion and enrichment of child development services through programs in different sectors. The focus of Eighth Five Year Plan (1992-97) was on human development through advocacy, mobilization and community empowerment. The Government declared its commitment to development of 'every child' which was manifested in the two National Plans of Action adopted in 1992, one for children and other exclusively for the girl child. The Ninth Plan (1997-2002) directed its efforts to expedite the effective implementation and achievement of the goals set in the two plans of action.

National Policy for Children

The national policy for children was adopted in 1974 with a view to provide adequate services to the children, both before and after birth and through the period of growth to ensure their full physical, mental and social development.

National Plan of Action for Children

The national plan of action for children 1992 has get goals for various indications for the year 2000 A.D., the achievements of the goals are in the process of review and fresh goal for the present decade is to be set.

National Nutrition Policy

The national policy was adopted in 1993 under the aegis of department of women and child development. The policy recognized the multifaceted problem of malnutrition and advocated a multisectoral approach for controlling the same. A series of action were identified in various spheres like food production and distribution, health and family welfare, agriculture, horticulture and rural development. In pursuance of this policy, the Food and Nutrition Board was transferred to this department on 1st April, 1993.

National Charter for Children

The national agenda for Governance enunciated the Government's intention to announce a National Charter for children with an aim to ensure that no child remains illiterate, hungry or lacks of medical facilities. The department prepared an approach paper on the National Charter for children and obtained of the views, comments and suggestions of the state Governments/UT Administrations and concerned Central ministers and departments. (Annual Reports, 2000-01 of Ministry of HRD, Govt. of India.)

Child labour is not unique in India. It is a universal phenomenon. Child labour always existed under different names. Children were always taken as additional help for domestic, agriculture, business or industrial work. The children are employed in gainful occupations because of three main reasons. Firstly, they belong to the families under the poverty line, so that it will be difficult for their parents of guardians to provide for the daily needs of the family without their supplementary income. Secondly, they come in for employment to gain some technical knowledge so that they become experts at an early stage. Thirdly, deficiency of the facilities for compulsory education also compelled parents to allow their children to work for gain.

The Government of India has taken various legislative and executive steps to mitigate the evils of child labour by making provisions for medical, educational, housing and recreational facilities and to regulate the condition of work of child labourer.

But a review of these schemes protecting the children who are the citizen of the nation, makes it clear that the existing statutory provisions in respect of their working conditions, medical, educational, housing and recreational facilities that help to develop the personally of a growing a personality, are quite inadequate.

In addition, India's most occupation viz, its agriculture where a considerable majority of children are employed has not been covered by the law relating to the child labour. Indian conditions to do not permit to prohibit the child labour totally because it will be injurious rather than good in the absence of possible alternatives. It is therefore realized that children who are not able to make education or training are to be engaged in work so that they will be saved from being misguided.

Adults Too Early

While in India Children's Day is celebrated on 14 November—the birthday of its first Prime Minister Jawaharlal Nehru who was exceedingly fond of children—universally it is celebrated on 20 November as it marks the anniversary of the day in 1959, when the United Nations General Assembly adopted the Declaration of the Rights of the Child

So far so good. But childhood innocence has now become something of a misnomer. Much to our amazement most children behave, talk and think like adults. This leapfrogging from childhood to adulthood with a momentary adolescent stopover gives serious cause for concern.

Social scientists cite myriad reasons for this rapid physiological, emotional and psychological growth. First, they blame the modern nuclear family system in which children are needlessly pampered. Doting dads and moms spoil their kids by not denying them access to satellite channels, the Internet and video parlors. Apart from film and gossip magazines, newspaper reports one eve teasing, rapes and molestations published with sickening regularity also arouse children's curiosity to explore sexual relationships. Sex education, introduced as a safeguard against AIDS or child abuse, contributes to their early maturity.

"It is a wise father that knows his child", said Shakespeare. But few parents do indeed bother to know their offspring. Take the case of the latchkey child who learns to "live without the constant solicitude of his mother, his nanny or his cradle-rocker. He grows up in the company of the housemaid, imitates her language and manners and enters the twilight zone of adulthood at a very early age. Pedophiles are on the prowl eve where—in educational institutions, places of worship and on sea beaches. Street children and child labourers are vulnerable to physical abuse and so their initiation into adulthood, too, starts early.

Roald Dahl, one of the bestselling British authors of children's books, in his celebrated poem *Television,* advises parents to install a lovely bookshelf in the wall instead of a television set and gill it with lots of books so that their children feel attracted to "fantastic tales of dragons, gypsies, queens and whales". According to him the "nauseating, foul, unclean and repulsive" television screen often keeps children hypnotized and drunk with "all that shocking ghastly junk". It "rots the sense in the head, kills imagination dead, clogs and clutters up and mind" turning them dull and imbecile with their powers of thinking rusting and freezing.

Reality shows are similarly detrimental to the future of children. Making girl participants wear skimpy and revealing clothes or putting adult language into their mouth defeat the very purpose of hosting such shows. In a Bangla dance reality show, girls aged between seven and 12 were found partnering grown up boys. The anchor—a boy paired with one girl or another—was often made to utter words of flirtations unbecoming of his age. It was sickening that the audience too split their sides soaking up the environment of a perverted thrill at the expense of two innocent children. The Shinjini case is a stern reminder that behind the glamour and glitz of reality shows lurks many a sordid tale. The grueling competition that promises instant fame and instant money—a distant mirage to the majority—leaves participants feeling shattered.

Shakespeare's description of the transition from the eternal "whining schoolboy, with his satchel creeping like snail/ Unwillingly to school" to the lover who sighs "like furnace with a woeful ballad" made to "his mistress' eyebrow" does not exactly conjure the image of a modern schoolboy who seems to be a much cleverer, intelligent and mature person walking his girlfriend home. No longer do people call such a school student a precocious little brat: the likes of him smoking cigarettes, ogling at the passing girls and talking without inhibition on subjects ranging from cricket to sex strut around everywhere.

The Supreme Court wants the government to stop obscenity and violence on the country's TV channels. The National Commission for Protection of Child Rights too has recommended that children below 16 years of age be barred from participating in reality shows. Even if implemented, the measures would not "bring children on the centrestage of development". The UNO, the UNICEF and other high-powered bodies should address this issue in right earnest.

(*Source* : "The Statesman", dated 18th November , 2008)

5.3 PRESENT SURVEY

(Field Survey to Highlight Law and its Practice in the State of West Bengal)

In the state of West Bengal the practice of the child labour is appalling. The unorganized sector and the rural area where agriculture is practiced witness almost ninety percent of work out put through utilization of child labourers. A random survey of various areas of the different districts within the state of West Bengal was carried out during the period of 2002-03 in order to make an assessment of the percentage of child labour being used by various establishment and organizations.

The problem of child labour has been attempted to be tackled by various legislative measures, policy inventions and initiatives by non-governmental organizations as well as by various international agencies working in the state of West Bengal. However, the recent past has been a witness to combat this problem at all levels—ranging from the grassroot at the village panchayat level to those by international agencies namely UNICEF and ILO (through its international programmes for the Elimination of child labour). Numerous efforts in the form and coverage making a significant dent to arrest the evil practice of child labour in West Bengal is bring run, however, there is a general feeling that most of these efforts have failed to realize its goal.

Before the details of the present study are speltout, it would be worthwhile to have a quick glance at the child labour situation in West Bengal. With a view to effectively dealing with the problem of child labour, efforts have to be made to understands its intricacies. This in turn is crucially dependent on being able to comprehend the problem from several angles. In fact, in the absence of proper comprehension of the problem, there is possibility that myopic actions may be taken losing sight of the multi-dimensional character of the problem. In such situations, the effectiveness may be lost and may be even retrograde to the welfare of children involved. A possible and realistic way of attacking the problem may be to examine the situation of working children in detail and magnitude of child labour in various parts of the West Bengal. This may pave the way for placing the problem in an appropriate perspective and framework amenable to future analysis and policy formulations.

According to the present experimental survey carried out by researcher, throughout West Bengal there are at least approximately 15 lakh children between the age of 5 and 14 who are fully at work, and more than 6 lakh of those for whom work is a secondary activity. West Bengal is one of the eleven states in India where 90 percent of child labour population is found. However, the estimates of the number of child workers vary in India because of the difference in the methodologically used to estimate child labour and also because of the conceptual differences regarding the definition of 'child labour' and 'work' itself.

If we analyse the above mentioned data of Table [5(3).2] it can very well be established that the statistics of West Bengal is the average sum total of the representations of all the districts of West Bengal. Therefore, the state of West Bengal nevertheless contributes a clean statistical percentage of the working children to the country's main stream statistics of working children.

During the random survey conducted throughout the state of West Bengal relating to the child labour it has been found that various factors are responsible to increase and decrease of the percentage of the working children, such factors being: (1) view of ruling party, (2) economic policy and market economy of the government, (3) literacy among the common people, (4) political and legal consciousness of people, (5) earning capacity of general masses, (6) the degree of poverty, (7) degree of urbanization, and (8) standard of education, etc.

Table 5(3).1
District-wise Establishment Showing Prevalence of Child Labour (W.B.)

Name of the District	Specific place of survey in the District	Establishment and process engaging child labour	Average percentage of child labour	Remarks (if any)
(1)	(2)	(3)	(4)	(5)
Burdwan	1. Asansol Raniganj and Associated coal belts of Eastern 2. Durgapur 3. Block Jamalpur 4. Block Bhatar 5. Block Galsi 6. Ausgram 7. Memari 8. Areas under Block Khandoghosh 9. Raina I and Raina II	Rice mills, Oil Mills and Milling operations, Brick fields and Brick making, Poultry, Hotels, Resturents, Agriculture Operations, Eating place and Stalls, Tea Stalls, Automobile Machinery Repairing Garages, Transportation works, Variety of Shops, Grill and Machinery, Manufacturing, Engineering Works, Shoe plants, Stone quarrying, Pharmaceutical Manufacturing, Chemical Product Manufacturing and Domestic child labour.	88	

Kolkata	Bagbazar, Tegra and Tiljala, Chetla, Dharmatala, Burrabazar, Kidderpore, Gerden Reach, Cossipore, Park Circus and Entally, Dumdum, Bowbazar, Ballygange, Alipure and Mominepore.	Big shops and Agency House, Packing, Table Processing, Leather Processing, Electronic Manufacturing, Ship Building, Transpiration Works, Idol Making and its Associated Works, Big Hotel and Restaurants and Ceramics.	84	Utilization of child labour as daily labours and in Household aids are eliminated from calculated.
Howrah	Dasnagar, Ghosapara, Ghusuri, Munshirhat, Santragachi, Chakarberisa, Shibpur, Uleberia, and its Associated Areas Amta, Andul, Liluah, Bally, Baltikuri, Chengail, Bakultala and Dankuni Area.	Automobile Reparing Works, Glasss Manufacturing, China Clay Works, Tanneries, Manufacture of Iron Products, Household Work, Soap, Match Fire Works, Plastics and Fibre Works, etc.	89	-Do-
Midnapore	Kharagpur, Contai, Tamluk, Digha, Kolaghat, Jhargram, Panskura, Goaltor, Kespur, Kona, Chaukola, Ghatal, Ballichak, Chandra and Midnapore Town.	Vegetable Production, Agriculture and Agricultural Operations, Timber Manufacturing and Supply, Hotels And Tourism Centers Thermal Power Supply, Foresty Works and Manufacture of Forest Product.	62	-Do-

(*Contd.*)

TABLE 5(3).1 (Contd.)

(1)	(2)	(3)	(4)	(5)
Purulia	Santaldih, Raghunatpur, Adra, Anara, Jhalda, Purulia Town.	Rail Workers through Contractors, power startion, Foresty Works, Agricultural and Agriculture Oprations, Lacculture and Manufacture of Lac Products, Tobacco Manufacturing and Preparation of its product, etc.	75	-Do-
Bankura	Bankura Town, Akui, Indas, Kenduadihi, Kenja, Kura, Megia, Patrasayer, Sonamukhi, Bishnupur.	Agriculture and Agricultural Operations Lacculture and Manufacture of Lac and clay Product, Cottage Industries, Bidi Manufacturing, etc.	83	-Do-
Murshidabad	Jangipur, Lalgola, Berhambpore, Kandi, Jalangi, Faraka, Dhuliyan, Doulatabad, Azimganj and Murshidabad Town itself.	Sericulture and Silk Product Manufacturing Khadi and Cottage Industries, Carpet Weaving, Fishery &Forestry Works, Agricultural Operations, etc.	87	-Do-
Birbhum	Saunthia, Tantipara, Narayanpur, Nalhari, Illam Bazar, Dubrajpur,Bolpur, Santiniketan, Bishnupur, Bakreswar and Suri Town etc.	Apiculture Operation, Cloth Weaving Power Station, Sericulture Works, Khadi and Cottage Industries, Store Quarries, Agricultural Operation, etc.	80	-Do-

Hooghly	Chandnagar, Gopinagar, Jangipara, Janai, Dhaniakhali, Dasghara, Champadanga, Bhanderhati, Bhadershwar, Baidyabati, Serampore, Chinsura and Hooghly, Arambagh, Bandal, Mogra and Bansberia, Tarakeshwar, etc.	Jaggery Works, Match Factories, Aluminum Factories, Soap Manufacturing, Plastic and Fiber Manufacturing , Cork Products, Idol Making, Metal Works, etc., Agro Products, Jute Manufacturing Cloth Weaving, Paper Manufacturing, and Agricultural Operations.	93	-Do-
North 24 Parganas	Kanchrapara and its associated Areas, Bangaon, Agarpara, Barasat, Basirhat, Naihati, Barrack pore.	Agriculture fertilizer food product, fishery opration, vegetable processing, etc.	92	-Do-
Nadia	Santipur, Samudragarh, Nabadwip, Matiari, Mohanpur, Karimur, Kalyani, Ranaghat, Krishnanagar, Dubulia, Bethudahari, Chanderghat etc.	Milling Industry Oils Mills, Large Scale refractory and Engineering Industries Earthen Works, Brass and other Metal Manufacturing, Cloth weaving & Textile Manufacturing, and Agriculture, etc.	82	-Do-
Malda	Narayanpur, Mothabari, Pakharia, Mangalbari, Malda Town Old Malda.	Mango Orchards and Manufacturing Products, Foresty and Production of Foresty product, Agriculture and Agricultural Operation, etc.	75	-Do-

(Contd.)

TABLE 5(3).1 (Contd.)

(1)	(2)	(3)	(4)	(5)
West Dinajpur	Raniganj, Balurghat and Bansihari.	Navigation works, Forestry and Fishery, Agriculture, etc.	75	-Do-
Cooch Behr	Alipurduar, Buxaduar, Nishiganj, Cooch Behar itself.	Timber production and Supply, Wooden Works, Bundh Building Operations, Tourist Spot and Hotel Industry, Transporation Foresty, Oprations and Manufacture of Forest Products and Tea Plantation works and Tea Processing and Packing Works, etc.	90	-Do-
Jalpaiguri	Haldibari, Maynaguri, Jaldhaka			
Darjeeling	Siliguri Bagdogra, Matigara, Darjeeling, Ghoom Kalimpong, Kuseong, Mirikete.			

TABLE 5(3).2
Year-wise Percentage of Child Labour (W.B.)

Year	*Average Percentage of child labour utilized in the state of West Bengal (approximately)*	*Remarks*
1990	92	The Increase and decrase of the percentage of the utilization of the child labour in influenced by the parameters mentioned in this chapter later.
1991	91.6	
1992	90	
1993	88	
1994	86.2	
1995	81.2	
1996	78.3	
1997	77.8	
1998	75.2	
1999	73.6	
2000	81.5	
2001	80.3	
2002	72.4	
2003	64.6	
2004	60.5	Projection as no data is found

It has been found that more or less in all the districts within the state of West Bengal, there is a balance of these factors but as owing to agricultural-based economy, the degree of urbanization is very low, more than 80% of the people are poor farmers thriving below the poverty line, hence, in spite the fact that :

(1) Ruling government being favourable to the common people and trying its best in all manner to arrest the practice of child labour.
(2) Ruling government attempting to liberalize the economic policies (specially after signing the GATT Agreement) by giving large subsidies and loans.

(3) The literacy percentage of the districts being fairly high (after the commencement of the literacy programme by the government).[4]

(4) People not being conscious both legally and politically, the poor parents and impoverished families are compelled much against their wishes to put forward their children to work before maturity to earn their daily bread.

Further, based on the fourteen years informative statistics of West Bengal Labour Ministry reports a comparative study of the utilization of the child labour (in various Government/Non-Govt. Organization, public, private other variery of small scale industries and other processes) within the state of West Bengal has been worked out which has been presented earlier in Table 5(3).2.

The researcher has collected information regarding age groups of the children working as child labour in four districts of West Bengal. Out of 785 cases found in the survey nearly one third of them (33.91%) are children below 10 years of age.

Their proportion is much higher (about 40% in Burdwan and Birbhum districts) and slightly lower (about 25% in the other areas of Bankura and Midnapur.)

---

4. Literacy enables people to know the consequence of his activities. Even basic literacy makes both the parents and children conscious to realize that low engaging their children in work at an immature age can not only bring uncalled for miseries in their family in near future but also to the country at large and so that can condemn this social evil. India has launched a new scheme of education for all by the year 2010. It is basically a project for the dissemination of elementary education in 9 to identified State with world bank aid. The scheme involves a total package that provides for the basic economic needs of the peoples also. For the country with the dubious distinction of having the largest number of illiterates in the world (about 281 million out of which 30% about illiterate and 21.87% out of school children) the project underlines a new dynamic approach. A present literacy drive has caught up in India in a big way. Close on the basis of Kerala's total literacy achievement is that of Burdwan district of West Bengal over 90% of the programmes launched in September, 1990.

TABLE 5(3).3
Age Distribution of Child Labour

Districts	*Working children below 10 years*	*Working children in the age group 10-14 years*	*Total*
Burdwan and Birbhum	168(41.90%)	233(58.10%)	401(100%)
Bankura and Midnapur	89(24.93%)	268(75.07%)	357 (100%)
Total	257 (31.91%)	501 (66.09%)	758(100%)

TABLE 5(3).4
Education among the Child Labour

Districts	*Literates*		*Illiterates*	*No. of Children*	*Total*
	Up to class V	*Above class V*			
Burdwan and Howrah	78	36	287(71.57%)	401(100%)	114 (28.43%)
Midnapur and Darjeeling	57	16	284 (79.55%)	357 (100%)	73 (20.45%)
Total	135	52	571(75.32%)	758 (100%)	187 (24.27%)

Lack of awareness in the parents and prevailing illiteracy among the children can be considered to contribute to child labour even more than poverty among the poor families who send their children to work. In the table given above, this is apparently (Table 5(3).4) indicated as about 75% of the child labourers were found to be completely illiterate. From the table it is also clear that the level of illiteracy is more or less in the same in both the pair of districts. Again among the literate, roughly one fourth level were found to have studied above standard V. Nearly three-fourth of them dropped out by class V which shows a very high drop-out rate. This high drop-out rate reflects the way in which poor families are marginalized by the disruption of their agricultures economy. The data in this table make it clear that schooling has to be strengthened for the vulnerable families.

TABLE 5(3).5
Caste Categories among the Working Children

Districts	*Name of Child Workers*	*SC*	*One*	*UC*	*Religious minority group (muslims)*
Burdwan	401 (100.00)	239 (56.61%)	133 (33.16%)	5 (1.25%)	24 (5.98%)
Birbhum	357 (100.00)	192 (53.86%)	142 (39.78%)	19 (5.32%)	4 (1.12%)
Total	758 (100.00)	431 (56.86%)	275 (36.28%)	24 (3.17%)	28 (3.69%)

SC = Scheduled Caste, OBC = Other Backward Class, UP = Upper Caste

There is a high incidence of child labour and a corresponding level of literacy among certain castes. An analysis of the table mentioned above, which groups such children by caste, shows this clearly. Nearly half of the cases of child labour came from 'Dalit castes' alone.

Given that these castes are only 56.61% of the total population in different areas of Burdwan district and 53.78% various areas of Birbhum as well as well as considering they constitute 54% (approx) of the population of the state, the number of child workers coming from communities nearly five times higher than these figures would indicate. All this suggests that dalits still remain outside the scope of development. In a way, this also implies that can an effort towards elimination or rehabilitation of child labour should first take up these caste categories as the main target group.

Another social group that produces child labour is the other backward class group (the OBC). The size of child labour population belonging to these castes is also about a third of the total number of cases which corresponds to their constituent size in the over all population of the state. The number of the muslim children found in this survey is small. Only 28 cases out of 758 which does not seem to correspond half of the total figure were found to be Muslims.

Table 5(3).6
Parental Income of Child Labour

Districts	*Parental average income (Rs.)*	*Average parental income, if father also happens to be a labour (Rs.)*
Burdwan	357.44	707.80
Birbhum	121.84	628.57
Midnapur	223.65	685.60
Bankura	198.55	702.38
Hooghly	212.45	848.60

Note : Wages received in kind and other earnings from agricultural work is not included.

An analysis into the parental income a very definite trend that father's labour status is also a marked phenomenon for nearly half the child workers.

To ascertain the family income some details of income were sought, particularly the wages earned in kind and other benefits from agricultural operations. Informations of gross monthly earnings was also taken. The computations made on family income in Burdwan district in case of 198 workers. In these families the father or both the parents remain in the village. On the other hand, if the father also happens to be a labour, the average parental income of such households is found to rise to Rs. 707.80. Similarly, in the districts of Birbhum where child workers are engaged mainly on agriculture on a large scale, the average parental income was found to be only Rs. 121.84 for 297 workers. In these families, too, the father or both parents remain in the village. However, in case of the 59 families where the father was also found to be a labour, the average family income turnout to be Rs. 628.57.

Unfortunately, the data on family size is lacking in the survey, there are only 20 cases where two brothers work as labourers. In such cases, it may lead to a little deflection with regards to the average family income found in the survey. It is also interesting to note that in areas under Birbhum districts all the child labour cases were found to work agriculture, domestic work and shops and other establishments.

TABLE 5(3).7
Working Hours of Child Labours

Districts	*Below 8 hours*	*Between 8 to 10 hours*	*Between 12 to 16 hours*	*Above 16 hours*	*Total*
Burdwan	17 (4.24%)	370 (92.27%)	10 (2.49%)	4 (1%)	401 (100%)
Birbhum	6 (1.68%)	165 (46.22%)	163 (45.66%)	23 (6.44%)	357 (100%)
Hooghly	8 (2.90%)	203 (49.48%)	150 (42.38%)	30 (8.30%)	391 (100%)
Purulia	7 (3.70%)	198 (47.30%)	205 (55%)	28 (8%)	438 (100%)
Total	38	936	528	85	1587

The concept of 'Bachpan Bachao Andoldan' is an apt description of the worst tragedy of child labour exploitation. Children who are supported to spend time in playing or learning ironically have to work as bread-earners, not only for themselves but also for the family, and that too after, much hard labour. It is also paradoxical that working hours for all kinds of wage work is restricted to fixed hours, but the exploitation of children's labour found to go far beyond these limits.

Sectors coming under the protective umbrella of labour laws are not exception, the benefits accrue only to the adult workers is the false plea that the child workers is prohibited to such jobs. The child workers engaged in industrial units such as mills and workshops are facing more problems with regards to hours to work. At least that could have been checked by the machinery of labour laws. The plight of the child worker in such is far worse than that of adult worker.

The above table shows this misery of the child worker. Eight hours of work for an adult an accepted norm in all establishments. But for child workers, it seems to be a norm only for a small fraction, as in only 20% cases this norms seems to be followed. From the same table, it also emerges that 10 hours of work to be the norm of more than half child workers of the total number of child workers covered in this survey. Even worse, nearly one-third of these children work for 12 to 16 hours a day. Moreover, the working hours of hotels servants, tea shop boys and even domestic servants are intolerably long.

TABLE 5(3).8
Monthly Income of Child Labour (Approx.)

Average for the whole region	*Average in Burdwan district*	*Average in Birbhum district*
Rs. 227.55	Rs. 211.43	Rs. 246.30

(earnings include only wage in money terms excluding the maintenance provided).

As table shows, the average child labour was found to be earnings slightly above Rs. 200 per month. This was estimated at Rs. 227.55 with a slight variation in above two districts. The wage rate also differ substantially depending on the work opportunity and the occupations. It is also seen that income are also on the higher side for child workers in other industrial and mechanical work units. Yet another sector where children are engaged is good number such as in small business, vegetables and fruits vending, as hawkers or as betel-shop owners, their income are also found relatively better enabling them to send a remittance up t o Rs. 300 per month. Almost the same earning also accrues to those working in traditional family service occupations such as hair cutting tailoring or carpentry in urban establishments.

In contrast child labour engaged in small establishments earn far less. These include those working in shops, hotels, tea shops, etc. and also domestic servants. In these occupations the wages range between Rs. 60 to Rs. 200 per month. But in a large number of cases, the net monthly wage is found to be around Rs. 100 only through this excludes the substance provided. The only group of child labour who does not receive even these meager wages is that of motor garage workers of those servicing in mechanical workshops. They are considered as apprentices for several years. They do not get even pocket money until they learn to operate machine independently and/or they get maturity to commence their own workshops.

This section of child labour is also found to be in the youngest age group 6 to 10 years age.

A little higher wage is earned by those working as casual labour in construction work, earth cutting or in brick-kilns, etc. they usually get half the wage of adult workers as observed, the availability of such work for child labour does not exceed 150 days in a year, so their average monthly income also does not go beyond Rs. 200. However longer working hours and the amount of labour required coupled with hazardous and poor conditions are the woes of child engaged in such work.

There are almost 250 to 350 million child workers in the world, and India has the distinction of having the largest number. According to the National Sample Survey, 1997, the number of child workers is placed at 30 million. Unofficial estimates vary from 60 to 150 million, of these 4 million are estimated to be in hazardous jobs. Approximately 90% of child workers are found in the state of Andhra Pradesh, Madhya Pradesh, Maharashtra, Uttar Pradesh, Karnataka, Tamilnadu, Bihar, Gujarat, Rajasthan, Orissa, West Bengal.

In West Bengal alone there are approximately fifteen lakhs child workers, of which Kolkata has 3 lakhs. The problem is massive. A survey has been conducted by researcher in various districts of West Bengal in order to make an assessment regarding child labour. It began with survey of Burdwan District in various towns like Asansol, Durgapur, Chittaranjan, Panagarh areas where child labour is widespread. The study reveals that:

(a) 34% children work due to pressure.
(b) 30% work due to parental pressure.
(c) 64% of the children work as they have nothing else to do as the schools are not very attractive and teaching condition are poor.
(d) Only 6% of the parents feel education as important development.

Group discussion and personal meetings were conducted with parents and employers. Fathers generally held the view that economic upliftment would reduce child labour. They also said that when children were idle it was essential to put them to work. Mother also seemed to agree with the view that poverty in the reason for children having to work. While some of them agreed that literacy did not help them to get jobs, others suggested that boarding schools are essential to ensure that children stay in school.

However, it is interesting to note the views of employers. They feel that the employment of children is an act of charity. They say that it was the parents who make a request to them to employ their children. Child labour is cheap and children are generally obedient so the employers are keen to employ children.

Constant meeting were also held with government officials like staffs if Ministry of Labour, West Bengal, Secretaries and Joint Secretaries in the Development of labour, to sensitise them to the justice of child labour.

In furtherance of an announcement made by Prime Minister on Independence Day, in 1994, towards the elimination of child labour, the *State–level Child Labour Advisory Board* in West Bengal had formulated a plan of action where in it:

(i) Conducted a survey to assess the actual number of child labour in the state;
(ii) Ensured enrolment and retention for five years of primary education;
(iii) Ensured adequate facilities and materials for improvement in the quality of education; and
(iv) To remove all children from hazardous occupation.

Effort are being made at various levels and in different spheres of life to ensure that there is general sense of awareness of life to ensure that there is a general sense of awareness among the people on child labour issue. As a result, we now see that in many communities where child labour was the general practice, parents are sending the children to school and taking a sense of pride in this.

Further, Schools are now more sympathetic to child workers who come to be enrolled in the schools. Enrolment in schools is picking up. Formal schools and colleges are running their own programme for awareness-building through exhibition, debates, and other such measures.

Central and State Governments are also showing their concern. Several announcements have been made to undertake to contribute towards elimination of child labour.

This experience shows that when all concerned, i.e. children, parents, local community, NGOs trade union leaders, employers and government join hands to fight against child labour, their efforts can produce positive results and children, the most vulnerable and valuable treasure, cease to be exploited by the system.

Interestingly, NGOs are working sharing ideas and programmes of action to increase their effectiveness. Cini- Asha at Kolkata. Children Welfare Organisation at Burdwan and NCLP at Burdwan founded by Ministry of Labour, Government of India have long campaigned for abolition of child labour. These organizations are working in their respective areas to combat practice of child labour.

Wherever child labour in a particular area become the object of public concern, especially when there is world-wide attention as in the case of the Jute Industry in Hooghly district and Tea Industry of Darjeeling district of West Bengal. The official response is to free some of the children and set-up a school of some sort of them. This *adhoc* and piecemeal approach quells the public outcry but may have little long-term impact on the lives of children and their families. In time in the situation that prevailed earlier is partially re-established as is happening in Siliguri and Jalpaiguri clearly, projects for former child labourers require not only an assured level of government finding and administrative support, but sustained NGO involvement. The analysis of data collected through empirical survey reveals alarming and appalling condition of children engaged in works leaving their education, etc. The reasons behind the whole system also show the inept handling of problem by the Governmental agencies.

Thus it can be solved by a concentrated effort administrative machineries of government departments, NGOs and Public Spirited persons within the legal framework of the country.

Voluntary and NGO Organization receiving donation from Labour Ministry

1. Karimpur Social Welfare Society, Nadia District.
2. Unemployed Young Workers Society, Burdwan.
3. Bagmari Youth Progressive Association, Kolkata.
4. Bhagra Diamond Club, Burdwan.
5. Tegganj Children Welfare Organisation, Burdwan.
6. Ikhupatrika Social Welfare Organistion, Dist., Midnapore.
7. Jan Siksha Prachar Kendra, Kolkata.
8. Society for Educational and Environmental Development (SEED), Howrah.

NGO's Committed for Elimination of Child Labour through International Effort, in West Bengal

1. Chamatagara Adiwasi Mahila Samity, Bankura District, 92-93-94-95.
2. The forum for Communities united in Service, (Struggle against child labour of slum in Kolkata & Howrah, 92-93).
3. The Institute of Psychological and Education Research, Kolkata.
   Elimination of Child Labour through Study of Planned Projects (92-93).
   To Educate Child Labour of Unorganised Sector, 94-95.
4. Vivekakanda Educational Society.
   (Progranme to Abolish Child Labour in Kolkata, 94-95).
   (Child Labour in Motor Workshops and their Education, 94-95).
5. Kolkata social Project.
   (i) To Shop Child Labour, 92-93,
   (ii) To Boost children to go to school (94-95).
6. Cini-Asha, Kolkata
   (i) Improvement in Working Condition of Child Labour of Kolkata, 92-93,
   (ii) To Eradicate Child Labour from Various Part of Kolkata, 94-95.
7. Prantik Jan Vikas, Kolkata
   (Compulsory Education for child Labourers of Slum-dwellers in Kolkata)

5.4. PROBLEM OF CHILD LABOUR IN INDIA IN SUMMARY FORM

Child Labour

Children need to grow in an environment that enables them to lead a life of freedom and dignity. Opportunities of education and training are to be provided for them to grow into worthy citizens. Unfortunately a large proportion of children are deprived of their basic rights. They are found working in various sectors of the economy particularly in the unorganized sector. Some of them are confined and beaten, reduced to slavery or denied freedom of movement thus making child labour a human rights issue and a developmental issue.

Definition of a Child

Article 1 of The United Nations Convention on the Rights of the Child defines a child as anyone below the age of eighteen years. The Child Labour (Prohibition and Regulation) Act, 1986 defines child as "a person who has not completed his fourteenth year of age."

Meaning of Child Labour

'Child labour' is defined as any work within or outside the family that involves time, energy, commitment, which affects the ability of a child to participate in leisure, play and educational activities. Such work impairs the health and development of a child.

According to the International Labour Organization, "child labour includes children pre-maturely leading adult lives, working long hours for low wages under conditions damaging to their health and to their physical and mental development." They are often separated from their families and deprived of meaningful education and training opportunities that would offer them a better future.

Rights of Children

The Convention on the Rights of the Child is the outcome of the effort of the international community to arrive at a standard to be followed by all countries in matters relating to children. In the words of the Convention, "in all actions concerning children. . . . The best interests of the child shall be a primary consideration." It lays emphasis on the fundamental freedoms and liberties of the individual, protection against discrimination, violence, abuse, neglect and exploitation as well as on the positive measures such as upbringing within the family and under parental care, access to health care, social security, education, and to rest and leisure.

Childhood is required to be a period of 'evolving capacities'—of the "development of the child's personality, talents and mental and physical abilities to their fullest potential", primarily through education. During this period, a child has a right "to a standard of living adequate for the child's physical, mental, spiritual, moral and social development."

The Convention establishes the right of the child to be an actor in his or her own development, to express opinions and to have them taken into account in the making of decisions relating to his or her life. In a number of areas, the Convention goes well beyond existing legal standards and practices. These include its provisions on—

The right to a name and nationality from birth :

- the right to a name and nationality from birth
- adoption
- the rights of disabled and refugee children
- the rights of those in trouble with the law

It protects children from all forms of exploitation, deals with the question of children of minority and indigenous groups and the problems or drug abuse and of neglect.

Basic to the development of the child are the right to express views in all matters affecting her or him and of their being given due weight, freedom of expression including right to information and ideas, freedom of thought, conscience and religion, as well as freedoms of association and of peaceful assembly. The child has a right to privacy, and to special protection and assistance provided by the Sate where the child is deprived of family environment.

As regards employment, the child, in view of his physical and mental immaturity, has a special right to be protected from "economic exploitation and from performing any work that is likely to be hazardous or to interfere with the child's education, or to be harmful to the child's health or physical, mental, spiritual, moral or social development." Article 35 seeks to protect children from trafficking in children for any purpose or in any form.

Child Labour—Denial of Rights

Child labour is a concrete manifestation of denial of rights of children. Working children are denied their right to survival and development, education, leisure and play, opportunity for developing their physical and mental talents, and protection from abuse and neglect.

Decisions relating to employment of children are often taken by adults having control over them, and not always with the concurrence of the children themselves, who under the human rights canons shave basic rights and freedoms comparable to adults, with due regard to their age and maturity and parental responsibility.

Worst Forms of Child Labour—Global Scenario

It is estimated that there are about 8.4 million children welfare engaged in worst forms of child labour. This includes trafficking 1.2 million, forced bonded labour 5.7 million, armed conflict 0.3 million, prostitution 1.8 million and illicit activities 0.6 million

(Source: International Labour Organization, 2002)

Magnitude of Child Labour in India

India has the largest number of child labourers in the world. Withdrawing them from work and ensuring their rehabilitation is a major challenge facing the country. The proportion of working children to the total labour force is however lower in India than in many other developing countries.

According to the 1991 census, the total number of children in the age group of 5-14 years was 203.3 million. Of this 11.28 million children were child workers (6.18 million boys and 5.10 million girls). 79.7 million children were neither at school nor at work and came under the category of "nowhere children".

All children in the age-group of 6-14 years, who should actually be in school but are out of school, are deemed to be *actual or potential child labourers*. Child labour in India is much of a rural phenomenon than urban. 90.87 per cent of the working children were found to be in the rural areas and 9.13 per cent were in the urban areas.

State-wise Distribution of Child Labour

The distribution of child labour in various states indicates a certain co-relation. States having a larger population living below the poverty line have a higher incidence of child labour. Consequently, higher incidence of child labour is accompanied by high dropout rates in schools.

State-wise Distribution of Child Labour

The distribution of child labour in various states indicates a certain co-relation. States having a larger population living below the poverty line have a higher incidence of child labour. Consequently higher indicates of child labour is accompanied by high dropout rates in schools.

Extent of Child Labour in India

States	*Percentage*
Andhra Pradesh	14.5
Uttar Pradesh	12.5
Madhya Pradesh	12.0
Maharashtra	9.5
Karnataka	8.7
Bihar	8.3
Rajasthan	6.9
West Bengal	6.3
Tamil Nadu	5.1
Gujarat	4.6
Orissa	4.0

Source : Census of India, 1991.

Causes of Child Labour

Child labour is inherent in the vicious circle of poverty, unemployment, under-employment and low wages. Three primary factors are responsible for this: inequitable distribution of resources, centralized and lopsided economy and the backward nature of agriculture.

Consequently, the main causes for child labour are:

- Ignorance of parents about consequences of child labour.
- Traditions of making children learn family skills.
- Absence of universal compulsory primary education.
- Social apathy towards child labour.
- Non-availability and non-accessibility of schools.
- Irrelevant and unattractive school curriculum.
- Preference of employers for children, as they constitute cheap labour.
- Unemployment and low family income.
- Migration to urban areas.
- Large families.
- Children supplement the income of the family.
- Occupational rigidities of caste system.
- Employment structure in unorganized sector.
- Ineffective enforcement of the legal provisions pertaining to child labour.

Reasons for Economic Exploitation of Children

Employers believe that children have some of the requisite qualities best suited to their industry. Employment of child labourers is considered to be economically viable because a child labourer puts in more hours as compared to an adult worker engaged in similar work for which the child gets paid comparatively low wages. They further believe that :

- Children are quick learners, and pick up skills in doing minute work. For example, in the carpet weaving industry, children are preferred for employment because of their fingers.
- They do not protest, as they are ignorant about their rights. Moreover, they do not absent themselves from work.

- Being gullible and innocent they can be easily manipulated.
- They are unable to bargain or determine their appropriate wages and hence are inexpensive.
- Being ignorant they do not realize the hazards of the job they are doing.
- They can be removed as and when their services are not required.
- Their maintenance cost is very low.

Forms of Child Labour

Children are Engaged

- As labourer in both unorganized and informal sectors, which do not come within the purview of the law.
- As migrant labourer from rural area to urban area.
- As bonded labourer pledged by the parent or guardian to the employer in lieu of debts or payments.

Sectors of the Economy in which Children Work

1. Manufacturing Sector

Children are engaged in various manufacturing processes of different home-based industries. Very often they work in sub-human conditions and exploitative situations. Some of these industries are :

- Brassware
- Lock
- Match and fire works
- Diamond cutting
- Gem polishing
- Glass and bangle making industry
- Carpet making stone quarries
- Brick kilns
- Sericulture-silk industry
- Beedi-making

2. *Agrarian Sector*

In rural areas children are engaged in agricultural and allied occupations as a part of family labour or as individual workers.

3. *Service Sector*

In the service sector, children form part of:

- Self-employed labour
- Invisible labour
- Wage-based employment

Adverse Effects of Child Labour on the Health of Children

Children work for long hours often in dangerous and unhealthy conditions and are exposed to lasting physical and psychological harm. They tend to develop—

- Respiratory problems such as asthma, tuberculosis.
- General weakness, stunted growth, body ache and joint pains.
- Poor eyesight and other eye problems such as watering, irritation and reddening of eyes.
- Loss of appetite.
- Tumors and burns.
- Disability by working on looms.
- Susceptibility to arthritis as they grow older.
- Mental disabilities.

Constitutional and Legal Safeguards

1. *Constitutional Provisions*

The framers of the Constitution of India realized that children are the most vulnerable section of society and thus are at the maximum risk of being economically exploited. In order to safeguard children against economic exploitation the Constitution makes the following provisions :

(i) Fundamental Rights

Article 21A :

Right to Education

"The State shall provide free and compulsory education to all children of the age of six to fourteen years in a manner as the State may, by law, determine."

Article 23(1)

Prohibition of traffic in human beings and forced labour

"Traffic in human beings and 'begar' and other similar forms of forced labour are prohibited and any contravention of this provision shall be an offence punishable in accordance with law."

Article 24:

Prohibition of employment of children in factories, etc.

"No child below the age of fourteen years shall be employed to work in any factory or mine or engaged in any other hazardous employment."

(ii) Directive Principles

Article 39:

Certain principles of policy to be followed by the State

The State shall, in particular, direct its policy towards securing.....

"(e) that the health and strength of workers, men and women, and the tender age of children are knot abused and that citizens are not forced by economic necessity to enter vocations unsuited to their age and strength;

(f) that children are given opportunities and facilities to develop in a healthy manner and in conditions of freedom and dignity and that childhood and youth are protected against exploitation and against moral and material abandonment."

Article 45:

Provision for early childhood care and education to children below the age of six years

"The State shall endeavour to provide early childhood care and education for all children until the age of six years."

In addition to the above, the Constitution contains the following Articles under the Directive Principles of State Policy. The Directive Principles are fundamental in the governance of our country and it is the duty of all the organs of the State to apply these principles.

Duty of Parent/Guardian towards the Child

Article 51A(k) on Fundamental Duties states that it shall be the duty of e very citizen of India, who is a parent or guardian to provide opportunities for education to his child or, as the case may be, ward between these of six and fourteen years.

2. Legislations

Based on the Constitutional provisions and the Directive Principles of State Policy, a number of legislations have been enacted from time to time. The following is the list of such legislations, which aim at elimination of child labour from hazardous industries and regulation of their conditions of employment in other non-hazardous occupations.

- Factories Act, 1948
- Plantation Labour Act, 1951
- Merchant Shipping Act, 1951
- Mines Act, 1952
- Motor Transport Workers Act, 1961
- Appreticeship Act, 1961
- Beedi and Cigar Workers (Conditions of Employment) Act, 1966
- The Bonded Labour System (Abolition) CT, 1976
- Child Labour (Prohibition and Regulation) Act, 1986

Salient Features of the Child Labour (Prohibition and Regulation) Act, 1986 :

The Act :

- Prohibits/bans the employment of any person who has not completed his fourteenth year of age in occupations and processes enlisted in Part A and B of the Schedule of the Act.
- Lays down a procedure to decide modifications to the Schedule of banned occupations or processes.
- Regulates conditions of work where children are not prohibited from working.
- Lays down enhanced penalties for employment of children in violation of the provisions of the Act and other Acts.

Section 14 of the Act provides for punishment up to 1 year (minimum being three months) or with fine up to Rs. 20000 (minimum being ten thousand) or with both, to one who employs or permits any child to work in contravention of provisions in Section 3.

Children employed in occupation and processes, not banned by the Act are regulated by the following provisions :

- A child shall not be required to work for more than six hours a day which shall be inclusive of his/her half an hour break.
- No child shall be permitted or required to work between 7 p.m. and 8 p.m.
- No child shall be required or permitted to work over-time.
- Every child shall get a weekly off.

There is an obligation on the part of the employer to furnish information to the inspector regarding the employment of children. It is mandatory for the employer to maintain a register on this matter.

3. *International Safeguards—Convention on the Rights of the Child*

India became a party to the Convention of the Rights of the Child, on 11 December 1992. The Convention gives substance to India's concern for the protection of the rights of children in all spheres, including protection from economic exploitation. As a signatory, India is under obligation to take the necessary legislative, administrative, social, and educational measures to ensure the implementation of the Convention.

Besides, India has ratified six ILO (International Labour Organisation) Conventions relating to child labour, three of them as early as the first quarter of the 20th Century. The International Labour Conference adopted a resolution on child labour in 1979. The resolution called for a combinaqtion of child labour and measures for humanizing child labour wherever the same cannot be eliminated outright.

The ILO through the Global Technical Co-operation on Child Labour known as the International Programme on the Elimination of Child Labour (IPEC) has been playing an important role in the process of gradual elimination of child labour and protection of children from industrial exploitation. It has focused its attention on five major issues :

1. Prohibition of Child Labour
2. Protecting Child Labour at work
3. Attacking the basic causes of child labour
4. Helping children to adopt to future work
5. Protecting the children of working parents.

In June 1999, the ILO adopted the Convention on the Worst Forms of Child Labour. This Convention addresses issues such as rehabilitation and social integration of child labourers.

United Nations International Children's Emergency Fund (UNICEF) acknowledges the importance of child labour prevention and elimination. It accordingly supports Government and civil society in their efforts to redress the needs and rights of all children.

4. *National Child Labour Policy*

Elimination of child labour demands sustained efforts over

a period of time. Enactment of child labour laws, rehabilitation of child labourand preventing entry of child to work should be part of the elimination strategy. Efforts should be made to improve the economic status of their parents through various anti-poverty and employment generation programmes.

The National Child Labour Policy, 1987 includes the following factors:

- Strict enforcement of the provisions of the Child Labour (Prohibition and Regulations) Act, 1986 and other concerned legislations.
- Rehabilitation of child withdrawn from employment.
- Reducing the incidence of child labour progressively.
- Providing better and readily accessible education, through formal or non-formal systems of education.
- Improving health conditions for child labourers.
- Providing nutrition through schemes like the "Integrated Child Development Services".
- Intensifying the anti-poverty programmes such as integrated rural development services.
- Focusing on areas known to have high concentration of child labour.
- Adapting a project approach to identity withdraw and rehabilitate working children.

The National Child Labour Projects (NCLP) launched in 1988 are time bound projects that seek to implement model programmes consisting of key elements such as :

- Stepping up the enforcement of the prohibition of child labour.
- Providing employment to parents of child labour.
- Expanding formal and non-formal education.
- Promoting school enrolment through various incentives, such as payment of stipend.
- Raising public awareness.
- Survey and evaluation.

The major activities undertaken under the NCLP are the establishment of special schools to provide non-formal health care, etc., vocational children withdrawn from employment 12 NCLPs were started in Andhra Pradesh (Jaggampet and Markapur), Bihar (Garwah), Madhya Pradesh (Mandasur), Maharashtra (Thane), Orissa (sambalpur), Rajasthan (Jaipur), Tamil Nadu (Sivakasi) and Utter Pradesh (Varanasi Mirazapur-Bhadoi, Aligarh and Firozabad).

In order to fulfil the constitutional mandate, a major programme was launched on 15 August 1994 to withdraw children working in hazardous occupations and to rehabilitate them thorough Special Schools. As a follow up, the Government constituted the National Authority for the Elimination of Child Labour (NACEL) on 26 September 1994. Its aim is :

- To formulate policies and programme for elimination of child labour.
- To monitor the progress of programmes, projects and schemes.
- To co-ordinate the implementation of child labour related projects of the concentrated Ministers of the Government of India.

Currently 100 projects are functioning in the children labour endemic states of the country.

5. Guidelines laid down by the Apex Court to eliminate Child Labour

The Supreme Court in *M.C. Mehta* v. *State of Tamil Nadu* (AIR 1997 SC 699) has taken certain pragmatic steps towards effective implementation of the policy. They are:

1. Survey for identification of working children.
2. Withdrawal of children working in hazardous industries and ensuring their education in appropriate institutions.
3. The offending employer must be asked to pay compensation of Rs. 20,000 for every child employed in contravention of the provisions of the Act. The liability of the employer would not cease even if he would disengage the child employed.
4. The sum so collected should be deposited in a fund to

be known as Child Labour Rehabilitation-*cum*-Welfare Fund. The Fund shall form a corpus whose income shall be used only for the concerned child. To generate income, the fund can be deposited in a high yielding scheme of any nationalized bank or other public body.

5. As the aforesaid income would not be enough to dissuade the parent/guardian to seek employment of the child, the State owes a duly to discharge its obligation. It should provide a job to an adult member of the family, whose child was employed in a hazardous industry.
6. In cases where it would not be possible to provide a job, the Government would, as it contribution grant deposits in the Child Labour Rehabilitation-*cum*-Welfare Fund a sum of Rs. 5000 for each child employed in a factory or mine or in other hazardous employment.
7. In either of the cases whether a job provided to an adult member of the child's family in lieu of the child or not, the child shall not be required to work.
8. In cases where alternative employment could not be made available as aforesaid, the parent/guardian of the concerned child would be paid the income, which would be earned of the corpus of Rs. 25,000 for each child every month. The employment given or payment made cease to be operative if the child would not be sent by the parent/guardian for education.
9. The National Labour Policy announced by the Government of India has already identified some industries for policy action.
10. A district could be the unit collection so that executive head of the district keeps a watchful eye on the work of the inspectors.
11. With respect to non-hazardous jobs, the inspectors shall have to see that the working hours of the children are not more than four to six hours a day and that they receive education at least for two hours each day. It would also be seen that the entire cost of education is borne by the employer.

The Ministry of Labour is monitoring the implementation of the directions of the Hon'ble Supreme Court.

Role of the National Human Rights Commission

The NHRC is deeply concerned about the employment of child labour in the country. The Commission has observed that even after fifty seven years of independence, child labour persists in the country. Despite various constitutional provisions, passing of legislations, becoming a party of international Conventions, announcement of a National Child Labour Policy, the constitution of National Authority for the Elimination of Child Labour and the undertaking of National Child Labour Projects, the goal of eradicating child labour remains elusive. Freeing the estimated two million children working hazardous industries by the year 2000 has not been achieved.

Hence the Commission focused the attention on the following industries wherefrom rampant reports of child labour received. These include:

- Bangle/Glass industry
- Silk industry
- Lock industry
- Stone Quarries
- Brick Kiln
- Diamond Cutting
- Ship-breaking
- Construction work
- Carpet-weaving

The Commission has been monitoring the child labour situation in the country through its Special Rapporteurs, visits by Members, sensitization programmes and workshops, launching projects, interaction with the industry associations and other concerned agencies, co-ordination with the State Governments and NGOs to ensure that adequate steps are taken to eradicate child labour. The Commission is specifically monitoring the carpet belt area in UP, the bangle/glass industry in Ferozabad and silk industry in Karnataka.

Unless the reality of free and compulsory education for all upto the completion of the age of 14 years is realized, the problem of child labour shall continue. To that the Commissions has involved the NGO sector in the non-formal education of child laboures. A number of such schools and training centers are functioning in the districts of the carpet belt. There has also been a distinct improvement in the level of awareness among the general public about child labour issues.

The Commission has been deeply concentrated about the employment of children below 14 years as domestic servants by Government employees. It took up the matter with the Central Government and State Governments to amend the Civil Services (Conduct) Rules prohibiting such employment. The relevant Civil Service (Conduct) Rules have been amended by Central Government and almost all the State governments to the effect that employment of children below the age of 14 years as domestic servants by Government employees shall be regarded as a misconduct inviting major penalty.

6

Conclusion and Suggestions

Children are the dawn for the future of a nation. Their protection and solitude are our responsibility. The planners of the country should keep a greater care in framing the policies for development of human resources, so that the growth of children be protected to make them goods citizens, physically fit mentally alert and morally healthy, endowed with skills and motivations needed by society. Equal opportunities for development of all children during the period of growth should be the main aim of the Government to carry out the programmes of socio-economic justice in India.

In any research it becomes obligatory on the part of the researcher to collect various findings of the data to make them useful for the public at large in general and children in our case particular. Findings given in a clear and concise form prove to be of considerable use to researcher as well as planners and policy-makers to implement the research objectives for betterment of children. This critical analysis on child Labour unveiled many roots of the problems relating to children and their surroundings.

But the establishment of U.N. in its historical retrospect the problem of child labour and abuse of the tender age children have been shown with minimal solutions generally in municipal laws and particular in a India. Internationally, although ILO started its quest to prevent exploitation of child labour effectively but the *Universal Declaration of Human Right* by the UN was the first most effective and sensitive move which received overwhelming global response not only in the field of children and child labour, but this declaration also paved the way for the universal observance of the respect for human dignity.

Gradually UN and its specialized agency ILO along with UNICEF and many NGOs (Non-Governmental Organisation) tried to do in planned manner for education of child labour with their shifting onus for global child welfare. Thereby, consequently Nation states of UN have made a large number of legal mechanism to arrest the menace of child labour to provide welfare and protection to children.

The problem of child labour is largely prevalent in the "Third World" or underdeveloped countries. India, a precursor of developing states and also as a welfare state could not give desired results on the issue of child welfare inspite of a tripartite protection relating to the welfare of the children and child labour during 55 years.

1. (a) Firstly, India is a Member of UN, so, internationally it observes the ILO standards in this matter and follows the directions of UN. It looks into its enforcement by means of legislation, regulations, rules and bye laws.

   (b) Secondly, citizens of India being conscious about this problem, the Government has framed various labour legislations which all aim to protect the interest to the child labour. These legislations which are not static but dynamic set of laws as those are legislations with new amendments come into force with changing times having penal and prosecution caluses on violation to make the citizens abide to these laws.

   (c) Finally, the Indian judiciary being the *protector liberator and caretaker* of the children, has not only balanced and given important decisions in many cases in favour of children but also has exercised the power of judicial review by checking the exercise of administrative discretion which violets the right of the child and child labour. In many cases it has judged the vires of the labour legislations and given direction for framing the laws so that they may not hamper the balance of interest. Recently the Indian judiciary has abolished the hindrance of the *locus standi* and has brought this social problem under the domain of Public Interest Litigation. It has not only given change to safeguard the interest of the children by public and social welfare spirited persons but also given a way out to the aggrieved to knock the doors of justice without any financial hurdles.

2. That the Government both in Center and States considering this problem as vital, are still trying to provide the welfare of the children and child labour in all respects. The needs of children and our duties towards them have been expressed in the Constitution. The Resolution on the *National Policy on Education,* adopted by parliament, gives direction to States policy on the educational needs of children. The goals set out in this document can reasonably be achieved by judicious and effective use of the available national resources. *Keeping in view of these goals, the Government of India, Department of Social Welfare has adopted the Resolution on the National policy for children on 22nd August, 1974. The SAARC Summit in New Delhi, 1995 was declared as the year of Poverty Alleviation targeting the goal to be attained by 2020. In this attempt, Compulsory education, integrated approach, law enforcement, employment generation and human resources development* are the programmes adopted by India to tackle the problem of child labour.
3. The problem of child labour exists in this country mainly because of widespread poverty and ignorance, and until these twin problems continue to exits, it will

not be possible to effectively tackle the problem of child labour. At present, India, it is impossible to eradicate totally poverty, illiteracy and child labour which are not only unrealistic but also likely would be more harmful than good to the millions of poverty stricken people in the country who are forced by their awfully poor economic conditions to seek the help of their children to make their both ends meet, Agriculture in this country is still the most predominant occupation engaging an overwhelming majority of the population. People depending upon agriculture are, barring a few, below the poverty line; and hence any step to ban labour in agriculture will aggravate their suffering rather than mitigating their problems. What seems to be realistic and pragmatic is to develop such conditions in which children, instead of being forced to make up employment, may be able to go to schools and pursue their studies effectively and in which those children who have unfortunately been driven to work, may also be able to start getting their education and to work in a healthy and congenial atmosphere in such a manner that their involvement in work does not bar their development of personality. In view of this object the following suggestions are provided for taking note of while considering the problem of child labour by all those who are interested on it :

1. Efforts should be made to demolish the problem of poverty from all sides by diligently implementing all developmental programmes directly concerned with promoting the interest of weaker sections in general and child labour in particular. Especially the *Integrated Rural Development Programme (IRDP), National Scheme of Training of Rural Youth for self-Employment (TRYCEM), National Rural Employment Programme (NREP), Rural Landless Labour Employment Guarantee Programme (RLRGP), Pilot Projects organized into Integrated Tribal Development Project (ITDP), Common Area Development (CAD)*

Programme, UNICEF associated scheme of Development of Women and Children and Rural Areas (DWCRA), etc. are to be enforced honestly to that the dream of founding fathers of the Constitucion to provide socio-economic justice to all, comes true.

2. Since many parents send their children in work because of not understanding and realizing the importance of education, it is necessary to inculcate the consciousness of education among them.
3. The Constitutional obligation to provide free and compulsory education to all children up to the age of fourteen years should be fulfilled without any further delay. It will be necessary to take the following steps for the fulfilment of this obligation:
   (a) Education should be made legally compulsory.
   (b) A group of educational institutions within easy access of children should be opened to cater education to the willing children within one kilometer redius of their residence.
   (c) Education up to 14 years without any discrimination based on sex, caste, religion, etc. should be provided free of cost.
   (d) The entire expenses on education of children should be shouldered by the Government.
   (e) The School curriculum environment and teaching method should be made attractive as well as interesting.
   (f) Social security programme of help to families with child labour to compensate the parents for the loss suffered by them for withdrawing of their children from work should be started.
   (g) *Community crèches* should be established to enable the child labour looking after the

young ones in their families, to attend the school.

(h) In case of child workers, who have never been to or left going to school, the Government should make it obligatory on their employers to bear all educational facilities/expenses to them.

4. Since some of the child workers have been destitute and *Ministry of HRD, Department of Women and Child Development, Government of India* has been keen running a scheme of assistance of Voluntary Organization through State Government for extending both institutional and non-institutional services to children up to 18 years of age to provide them care and protection, there is necessary for giving preference to voluntary organization coming forward to take up this scheme in rural areas. But it should be seen that NGOs must be genuine and not false or colourable.
5. Minimum Wages Act should be suitably amended to enhance the punishment for defaulters who are no paying wages to child workers.
6. The Government should initiate a dialogue with Trade Union at its earliest in order to prepare the institutional framework necessary for collective bargaining with regard to improvement in working conditions and to control the magnitude of child labour.
7. A comprehensive rural health care system based on a combination of preventive, promotive and curative measures starting at the village as a base should be built up.
8. Minimum Needs Programme with all its components of elementary education, rural health, rural water supply, rural roads, rural electrification, housing, assistance to rural landless labourers and nutrition should be effectively implemented.

9. Roads should be constructed or repair to link the village with towns for proper communication and upgradation of villages.
10. *Village Pradhans* should be given order to prepare a register of child labour at the village level, to send annual repost to this Block Development Officers highlighted the magnitude and condition of child labour and protect and promote their interest.
11. *The National Children's Boards, State Children's Board* should take more stringent to improve the lot,of child workers by identifying the hazardous employment and operation to stop their exploitation.
12. Seminars, Symposia, Discussions, etc. on various aspects of child labour should be organized from time to time and the problem of child labour should be widely published through different types of mass-media to create awareness among people about this social evil and to motivate them for coming forward eliminate it. So finally it can be suggested that the government should be care the latches and lacunas of legislations relating to child labour to endure their proper enforcement e.g.
    (i) Although India has ratified the UN Convention on the rights of child, but it is still to carry its principles into effect.
    (ii) India has still not ratified the ILO convention of 1973, which provides a minimum age of employment for children.
    (iii) Most of the child labour legislation confers power to statutory authorities under the statutes, with a little to the judiciary to safeguard the rights to the child etc.
    (iv) Finally, the citizens of our country should be dutiful to protect the rights of child by showing strict and proper adherence to the child labour laws and child welfare legislations of our country and taking active participation in arresting this social evil.

APPENDIX A

QUESTIONNAIRE

In India, still the problem of Child Labour is alarming. There are various reasons such as, poverty, illiteracy, etc. for the problem. The researcher has undertaken a research project leading to Ph.D. degree in law at Burdwan University to analyse various legal issues related with the problem. An empirical survey on Child Labour is undertaken within West Bengal or to explore the real reasons pertaining to the problem which still is beyond solution by the planners of the country. It was quite impossible for the researcher to conduct empirical survey throughout whole India.

Therefore in the Eastern-Zone of the Country the West Bengal will be area of sample survey. The questionnaire is forwarded to you for knowing certain informations. Kindly answer to help the undersigned. Your views shall be kept strictly confidential.

With regards,

Yours Faithfully,

DIPAK DAS

1. What group Children are engaged as labour?
2. Where do they work?
3. What is their nature of work? (Kindly tick against right answer)?
   Agricultural/Domestic/Hotels and Restaurant/Shoepolish/Garrages/Any other.
4. What is occupation of Child's father?
5. How many members are there in his family?
6. What are reasons behind his engagement as child labour?
7. Whether he goes to school ? if yes, in which class he reads?
8. Whether he is working as labour beyond school hours?
9. What is education of his parents?
10. What is the religion or caste of child labour?
11. Whether he is engaged in labour against his will?
12. How much he is earning per day (minimum wage)?
13. What is duration of his work? (Kindly put a tick mark in right answer) 20/25/12/18/6/4 hours?
14. Whether the nature of work frequently changes in a year?
15. How is Climatic/Geographical condition of the place where he resides? Whether that is responsible for engaging him/her into such system?
16. What should be the steps to ameliorate their condition or to eradicate this social menace?
17. What are the measures adopted by Govt./Non-Govt. Organizations to help child labour?
18. Do you know about some Govt./Semi-Governmental organizations busy to change their plight?
19. Do you favour the eradication of child labour?
20. What is your overall opinion regarding problem of Child Labour?

Date :

Name :
Designation :
Address :
Occupation :

APPENDIX A

SCHEDULE

In India, still the problem of Child Labour is alarming. There are various reasons such as, poverty, illiteracy, etc. for the problem. The researcher has undertaken a research project leading to Ph.D. degree in law at Burdwan University to analyse various legal issues related with the problem. An empirical survey on Child Labour is undertaken within West Bengal or to explore the real reason pertaining to the problem which still is beyond solution by the planners of the country. It was quite impossible for the researcher to conduct empirical survey throughout whole India.

Therefore, in the Eastern-Zone of the Country the West Bengal will be area of sample survey. The schedule is forwarded to you for knowing certain informations. Kindly answer to help undersigned. Your views shall be kept strictly confidential.

With regards,

Yours Faithfully,

DIPAK DAS

1. What is your age?
2. Where do you work?
3. What is the nature of your work?
4. Who are the members of your family?
5. What is the total number of members in your family?
6. Why are you working?
7. How far have your parents studied?
8. Do you go to school?
9. After the school what kind of work do you do?
10. What is your religion?
11. Are you related with family profession?
12. Are you doing something which ancestors have done?
13. What is your minimum wage?
14. What is the daily duties of work in hours—12/20/15/8/6
15. Does the nature of your work change frequently or it remains the same all through the year?
16. What is the importance of the atmosphere, location, or family on condition of your work?
17. Do you like this work?
18. What are measures to liberate you or what may be done to facilitate your liberation from this condition?
19. What steps have been taken by the government for helping the child labour?
20. What measures have been adopted by various governments and NGO's for the upliftment of child labour?

Name of Child labour :
Place of work :
Caste/Religion :
Date :
Address :

List of Cases

1. Andhra State Financial Corporation *v.* Gar Re. Rolling Mills 1994(2) SCC647:AIR 1994 SC, 2151, 101
2. Anand Vardhan Chandel *v.* University of Delhi, AIR 1978 Delhi, 308, 109
3. Air India Statutory Corporation *v.* United Labour Union, AIR 1997, SC 645, 63
4. Bandhua Mukti *v.* Union of India, AIR 1984, SC, 802, 102, 113
5. B. Banerjee *v.* Smt. Anit Pan, AIR 1975, SC, 1146, 106
6. B.L. Wadhera *v.* Union of India, HC CWP 1796/1999, 115
7. B.L. Wadhera *v.* Union of India, HC CWP 266/2000, 115
8. B.L. Wadhera *v.* Union of India, HC CWP 3774/2001, 115
9. B.L. Wadhera *v.* Union of India, AIR 2002(2) SC, 350 Para 75, 115
10. B.L. Wadhera *v.* Union of India, HC (Ranchi) WPC (PIL) No. 3482/2002, 115
11. Bihar Legal Support *v.* The Chief Justice of India and others, AIR 1987 SC 38, 117
12. Dr. B.K. Subha Rao *v.* Mr. K. Prasaran, 1996(7) JT 265: 1996 Cr. L.J. 3983, 101
13. District Beedi Workers Union *v.* State of Tamil Nadu & Others, W.P. (Civil) No. 13064 of 1983 of SC, 124
14. Fertilizer Corporation Kamgar Union *v.* Union of India. AIR 1981 SC 344, 102
15. G. Narain Swami Reddy *v.* Govt. of Karnataka, AIR 1991 SC 1726 (1991 AIR SCW 1755), 101
16. Gaurav Jain *v.* Union of India, AIR 1990 SC 292, 102
17. Indira Gandhi Nahru *v.* Raj Narayan, AIR 1975, 98

Bibliography

Statutes

The Apprentices Act, 1961.
The Beedi and Cigar Workers (Conditions of Employment) Act, 1966.
The Bengal Juvenile Smoking Act, 1919.
The Child Labour (Prohibition and Regulation) Act, 1986.
The Child Labour (Withdrawal From Employment) Act, 1988.
The Child Marriage Restraint Act, 1929.
The Children (Pledging of Labour) Act, 1933.
The Children Act, 1960.
The Children's Code Bill, 2000.
The Code of Civil Procedure—Order 32.
The Code of Criminal Procedure—Sec 125, 360.
The Constitution of India, 1950.
The Employment of Children Act, 1938.
The Factories Act, 1934.
The Factories Act, 1948 and Other Labour Legislations.
The Guardians & Wards Act, 1890.
The Hindu Marriage Act, 1955.
The Hindu Minority and Guardianship Act, 1956.
The Hindu Succession Act, 1956.
The Indian Contract Act, 1872.
The Indian Divorce Act, 1869, As Amendment in 2001.
The Indian Factories Act, 1891.
The Indian Succession Act, 1925.
The Inland Steam Vessels Act, 1917.

The Juvenile Justice Act, 1986.
The Merchant Shipping Act, 1958.
The Mines Act, 1904.
The Mines Act, 1952.
The Motor Transport Workers Act, 1951.
The Orphanages and Other Charitable Homes Supervisions and Control Act, 1960.
The Parsee Marriage and Divorce Act, 1936.
The Plantation Labour Act, 1951.
The Probation of Offenders Act, 1958.
The Protection of Human Rights Act, 1993.
The Shops and Establishment Act.
The Special Marriage Act, 1954.
The Tea District Emigrant Labour Act, 1926.
The Indian Mines (Amendment) Act, 1935.
The West Bengal Children Act, 1959.
The West Bengal Urban Primary Education Act, 1963.

Rules

Child Labour (Prohibition And Regulation) Rules, 1988.
Kerala Child Labour (Prohibition And Regulation) Rules, 1933.
M.P. Child Labour (Prohibition And Regulation) Rules, 1993.
Orissa Child Labour (Prohibition And Regulation) Rules, 1994.
Tamil Nadu Child Labour (Prohibition and Regulation) Rules, 1994.

Conventions

Minimum Age (Industry) Convention, 1919.
Minimum Age (Sea) Convention, 1920.
Medical Examination of Young Person (Sea) Convention, 1921.
Minimum Age (Agriculture) Convention, 1921.
Minimum Age (Trimmers and Stokers) Convention, 1921.
Minimum Age (Sea) Convention (Revised), 1936.
Minimum Age (Sea) Convention (Revised), 1936.
Minimum Age (Industry Convention), 1937.
Medical Examination of Young Person (Non-Industrial Occupations) Convention, 1946.
Medical Examination of Young Persons (Underground Work) Convention, 1965.
Minimum Age (Underground Work) Convention, 1965.

Medical Examination of Young Persons (Industry) Convention, 1946.
Minimum Age Convention, 1973 (24-15 & 31).
Night Work of Young Persons (Industry) Convention, 1919.
Night Work of Young Persons (Industry) Convention (Revised), 1945.
Night Work of Young Persons (Non-Industrial Occupations) Convention, 1946.
'Rights of the Child', CRC/C/15 Add. 115, 23, Feb. 2000.

Recommendations (ILO)

Minimum Age (Non-Industrial Employment Recommendations), 1932.
Minimum Age (Family Undertaking Recommendation), 1937.
Minimum Age (Underground Work) Recommendation, 1965.
Minimum Age (Coal Mines) Recommendation, 1953.
Minimum Age (Underground Work) Recommendation, 1965.
Minimum Age Recommendation, 1973.

Declaration

Declaration of The Rights of the Child, 1959

Reports (Govt. and Pvt.)

Annual Report 1999-2000, Department of Women and Child Development, Ministry of Human Resource Development, Govt. of India.
Annual Report 2000-01, Department of Women and Child Development, Ministry of Human Resource Development, Govt. of India.
Annual Report 2000-01, Ministry of Rural Development, Government of India.
Annual Report 1999-2000, V.V. Giri National Labour Institute, Sector-24, Noida (U.P.)
ASHA-CINI, *"Our Present Understanding of Child Labour Issues"*, The Administrator, 1996, New Age International (Pvt.) Ltd., New Delhi
Integrated Child Development Services, *Department of Women and Child Development*, Ministry of Human Resource Development, Govt. of India.

Juyal, B.N., *"Field From Bihar and Rajasthan"*, The Administrator, The New Age International (Pvt.) Ltd., New Delhi

Krishnan, L., *"Child Labour of Shivakasi"*, 'The Administrator'—1996, New Age International (Pvt.) Ltd. New Delhi.

Ministry of Labour, *"A Year of Major Achievements"*, 2001, Govt. of India, Shram Shakti Bhawan, New Delhi.

Report (Seminar) *"Child Labour and Their Rehabilitation" : Some Issues*, Himalayan and Central Asian Studies Vol. 4, No. 2, April-June, 2000

Sasnagi Santosh *"Child Labour in Angual District"*, The Administrator, 1996, New Age International (Pvt.) Ltd., New Delhi.

Books

Bellany Carol, *"The State of the World's Children-2001"*, Unicef Country Office, Indian Habitat Center, New Delhi.

B.R. Publication, *"Dimensions and Policy Options"*, 1993, New Delhi.

Chakarbarty, B., *"Education and Child Labour"*, 1989, Chugh Publication, Allahabad.

Freeman Michael, *"Children's Rights: A Comparative Perspective"* University of London, Darmouth (Aldershot, Bookfield USA, Singapur, Sydney).

Fyfe Alec, *"Child Labour"*, 2002, Policy Press.

Gathia, J.A., *"Women and Child Workers in Unorganized Sector"*, 1983, Concept Publishing Co., New Delhi.

Gupta, M., *"Young Hands at Work"*, Child Labour in India, 1987, Atma Ram Publication, New Delhi.

Giri, V.V., *"Labour Problem in Indian Industry"*, 1972, Asia Publishing House, Bombay.

George Ivy, *"Child Labour and Child Work"*, 1990, Ashish Publishing House, New Delhi.

ICSSR *"Data on Child Labour"*, 2002, Indian Council of Social Science Research, JNU, New Delhi.

Jain Hahaveer, *"Mannual for Trainers: of Enforcement Officials in Child Labour Legislation"* 2001, V.V. Giri National Labour Institute Sector, 24, Noida.

Jayaraj, D., *"Economics of Child Labour and Fertility"*, 1993, B.S.B.R. Publication, Delhi.

Jain, S.N., *"Child and Law"*, 1979, Atma Ram Publication, New Delhi.

Khulshrestha, J.C., *"Child Labour in India"*, 1978, Ashish Publishing House, New Delhi.

Krishna Suni, *"Restoring Childhood"*, Learning, Labour and Gender in South Asia, 2003, Konark Publications Pvt. Ltd.

Khatu, K.K., *"Working Children in India"*, 1993, Operational Research Group, Baroda.

Kan Bargi Remesh, *"Child Labour in the Indian Subcontinent"*, 1999, Sage Publications, New Delhi.

Mustafa, Mohd and Sharma, Onkar, *"Child Labour in India"*, 1998, Bitter Truth, Deep and Deep Publication, New Delhi.

Mendcliesich, *"Children at Work"*, 2001, International Labour Office, Geneva.

Mishra, Lakhmidhar, *"Child Labour in India"*, 2000, Oxford University Press, YMCA, Library Building, Singh Road New Delhi-110001.

Mehta, P.L. and S.S. Jaswal, *"Child Labour and the Law"*, 1998, Myth and Reality of Welfare Measures, Deep and Deep Publications, New Delhi.

Mehaveer Jain, *"Child Labour in India"*, 1987, National Labour Institute, Noida.

Mishra, Lakshmidhar, *"Bharat mein bal Majoor"* (Hindi), 2000 Deskal Publication.

Memoria, C.B. and Joshi, C.L., "Labour Problems and Social Welfare in India", 1996, Kitab Mahal Pvt. Ltd., Allahabad.

Mitthal, Mukta, *"Child Labour in Unorganized Sector"*, 1974, Anmol Publications Pvt. Ltd., New Delhi.

Nazir Ahmed Shah, *"Child Labour in India"*, 1992, Anmol Publications Pvt. Ltd., New Delhi.

Nangia, Preveen, *"Child Labour" : Cause Effect Syndrome*, 1987, Janak Publications, New Delhi.

Preetha Joshi, *"International Labour Organization and its Impact on India"*, 1985, B.R. Publishing Corp., Delhi.

Pati, R.N., *"Rehabilitation of Child Labour in India"*, 1991, Ashish Publishing House, New Delhi.

Patil, B.R., *"Working Children in Urban India"*, 1998, D.B. Publishers, Bangalore.

Rao, G. Lakshmi, *"Child Labour" : The Harsh Reality Jaripata*, Nagpur.

Rogers Gerray and Gury Standing, *"Child Work, Poverty and Underdevelopment"*, 2001, International Labour Office, Geneva.

Singh, Surendra and Raj Bhadur Singh Verma, *"Child Labour in Agriculture"*, 1987, Printing House (India), Lucknow.

Sunmangala, M., Nagarajun, B.S., *"Economics of Child Labour and Fertility"*, 1993 , B.R. Publishing Corp., Delhi.

Singh, I.S., *"Child Labour"*, 1992, BH Publishing Co. Pvt. Ltd., New Delhi

Tripathy, S.N., *"Migrant Child Labour in India"*, 1973, The World Book of Encyclopedia, Vol. 3, Field Enterprises Educational Corporation House, Chicago.

Tripathy, S.N., *"Exploitation of child Labour in Tribal India"*, 1991, Daya Publishing House, Delhi.

UNICEF, *"Children", The Epiccentre of Recovery*, Country Office, Indian Habitat Centre, New Delhi.

V.V. Giri National Labour Institute *"Bal Shram Kanoon", Ek Awalokan*, 2000, Sector 24, Noida.

V.V. Giri National Labour Institute, *"Child Labour in India"—An Overview*, 2000.

V.V. Giri National Labour Institute, *"Tools for Convergence", A National Perspective*, 1974-99.

Varandani, G., *"Child Labour and Women Workers"*, 1998, Ashish Publishing House, New Delhi.

Weiner, Mayron, *"The Child and the State in India"*, 1991, Oxford University Press.

Wadehra, B.L., *"Public Interest Litigation"*, A Hand Book, 2003, Universal Law Publishing Co. Pvt. Ltd.

Journals

"Award Digest", *Journals of Labour Legislation Special Issue*— V.V. Giri National Labour Institute, Sector-24, Noida.

"Bal Shrampar Niyojakon Ki Pustika" (Hindi), 1978, ILO, PHD and IOE.

"Child Labour Challenge and Response"—2001, V.V. Giri National Labour Institute, Noida.

"Determinants Rural Wages : An Inquiry Across Occupations, 2004, Babu, P. Ramesh, J. Jeyaranjan, A.C. Nambiar.

"Child Labour in Buland Shahar, District of Uttar Pradesh", Tapan Kr. Panchal, NLI Research Studies Series (No. 14/ 2000).

V.V. Giri National Labour Institute, "Children of Carpet Looms", A Study of Home-based Production of Carpet in Utter Pradesh NLI Research Studies Series (No. 011/2000).

Ravi, S. Srivstava and Nikhil Raj, "Processing of the Care Group Meeting" October 25, 1997, V.V. Giri National Labour Institute, Noida.

"Right of Workers", *Journal of Institute of the Human Rights,* Dr. Rao, G. Lahmi.

"Proceeding of Meeting of NGOs, Trade Unions and Enforcement Officers", May 8, 1998, Child Labour Legal Studies Cell, V.V. Giri National Labour Institute, Noida.

"Showing the Way-Trade Unions against Child Labour in India, 1998, ILO Area Office for India Habitat Centre, Lodhi Road, New Delhi.

"Rastron Ki Pragati" (Hindi), 1999, UNICEF, 73, Lodhi Estate, New Delhi.

Duniya Ke Bachhao Ki Estithi (Hindi), 2001, UNICEF (Country Office), 73, Lodhi Estate, New Delhi.

Midia aur Bal Adhikar, 2000, Unicef, "Workshop of District Collectors and Project Directors on Child Labour", V.V. Giri National Labour Institute, Noida.

Articles

Mudha, P., *"National Child Labour Project in Tiruchirapalli"*, 1996 (Jul-Sept.) 41 Adm. 163-8.

Apporva, *"Child labour Scenario in North Arcot Ambedkar District"*, 1996 (July-Sept.) 41 Adm. 151-58.

Agnivesh Swami, *"Ratification of Convention mere Window Dressing", Mainstream,* Oct-2, 1993.

Anand, R.K., "International Environment Law and Agenda", 21 Rio Declaration, Souvenir ILI, 1994.

Baxi, Upendra, "Unconditional Politics and Child Labour", *Mainstream*, Oct. 2, 1993.

Bachman, S.L., "A New Economic of Child Labour", Searching for Answers Behind the Headlines", 53, No. 2, *Journal of International Affairs,* "Spring", 2000.

Bakshi, P.M., Air Pollution and Child Health : Legislation and its Enforcement, Souvenir, ILI, 1994.

Bhat, P. Iswara, *"Legal Management of Ground Water to Ensure Rational use and Development with Justice"*, Souvenir, ILI, 1994.

Bashin, Lalit, *"The Problem of Child Labour and Lack of Primary Education in India"*, Souvenir, ILI, 1994.

Cini-Asha, *"Our Present Understanding of Child Labour Issue"*, 1996 (July-Sept.) 41 Adm. 189-76.

"Convention on the Rights of Child", 1997 (AP) : 12 Law Col. 28-9.

Clements Miliard, *"Three Realities that Challenges Health and Workers Environments, Lawyers, Political Leaders and Children Today"*, Souvenir, ILI, 1994.

Calla, M.R., *"Law relating to custody of minor children in India and hazards to Human Health Life with reference to environment in India"*, Souvenir, ILI, 1994.

Chopra, R.K, *Environment Health*, Souvenir, ILI, 1994.

Desai, A. Ashok, *"Juris Environmental Prudence"*, Souvenir, ILI, 1994.

Desai, Nishtha, *"Paedophilia is Goa after Freddy Peat"*, 1997 (May) 12 Law Col. 22-25.

Dixit, J.N., *"Govt. Promoting Rights to the Child"*, Mainstream, Oct-2, 1993.

Deb, L.K., "Child Labour Problems and Prospects": A Socio-Legal Analysis, 1998 (N) : 31 lab IC 181-6.

Govt. of India, *"India's Accession to the Convention on the Rights of the Child"*, Mainstream, Oct. 2, 1993.

Goswami, V.G.,•*"Impact of UN Conventions on the Rights of the Child Labour in India"*—A Socio Juridical Approach, 1 Luck ULI 55-65.

Hanumantha, K. Rao and Madhusudan M. Rao, *"Employers View of Child Labour"*, 1998 (JL): 34 IJIR 15-38.

ILO Policy, *"Towards the Abolition of Child Labour: 1999, ILO Policy and its Implications for ILO Technical Co-operation Activities"*, ILO Country Office, India Habitat Center, New Delhi.

Iyer Krishna, V.R., "Jurirprudence of Juvenile Justice"—A Preambular Perspective, Souvenir, ILI, 1994.

Jain, Mahaveer, *"List of Districts for Coverage under the National Child Labour Project (NCLP)"*, 1996 (July-Sept.): 41 Adm. 229-30.

Khanna, P., V.S. Kulkarni, *"Policy Option for Environmentally Sound Technology in India"* Souvenir ILI, 1994.

Munijal Rakesh, "Environmental Consumerism: its Imperativeness for Sub-continent in Global Context", Souvenir, ILI, 1994.

Mohammad, Ali Rather, *"Child Labour in Carpet Industry of Kasmir"*, Himalayan and Central Asian Studies, Vol. 4, No. 2, April-June, 2000.

Mehta, P.L. and Surender Singh Jaswal, *"Constitutional Philosophy of Child Labour Welfare"*, 1994, 1995 and 1996, 9, 10, 11 Kan L.J. 103-10.

Mahalwar, K.P.S., *"Legal Control of Untreated Sewage in India"*, Souvenir, ILI, 1994.

Maheswara Swamy, N. *"The Menance of Child Labour—Some Reasons and Reformations"*, 1997 (Jan.), 84 An. LT 1-4.

Nayak, R.K., *"Conservation of Humanity and Environmental Consumerism"*, Souvenir, ILI, 1994.

Porter George, *"Environment and the Law—Some Basic Issues"*, Souvenir ILI, 1994.

Pathak Gopal, Jha Janardan, "Small and Micro-Hydel Power Plants to the Rescue", Souvenir, ILI, 1994.

Prakas, N., *"Homes as dens for Child Labour"*, 1998 (May) 13 Law, Col. 28-9.

Patnail, V. and Singh, Joginder, *"A Select Bibliography on Child Labour"*, 1996 (Jul.-Sep.) 41 Adm. 231-48.

Pandit, Nirmala, *"Comparative Analysis of Provisions of the U.N. Convention on the Right of the Child and the Indian Laws"*, "The Administrator, 1996, New Age International (Pvt.) Ltd., New Delhi.

Priya, Vishnu, *"The UN Convention on the Rights of the Child 1989 Towards a New World Order"*, Souvenir, ILI, 1994.

Raj, Nikhil, *"Let us Converge to Eliminate Child Labour"*, Associate Fellow and Co-ordination, NRCCL, VVGNLI, Noida.

"Role of Education in Reducing Child Labour", Journal of Bio Sc. 32(3), 301-13, July, 2000.

Ramachandram, Sadhana, *"Rights of the Working Child in India: Law, Policy and Enforcement"*, Consultant, Legal Studies Cell, VVGNLI.

Rosencreanz, Armin, *"Recent Developments in International Environmental Law and Rights of Children, to a Clean Environment"*, Souvenir, ILI 1994.

Rudi, *"Some Remarks Regarding Child Labour in India"*, 'The Administrator'—1996, New Age International (Pvt.) Ltd., New Delhi.

Savya, Saachi, *"Children and our Future"*, 'The Administrator; 1996, New Age International (Pvt.) Ltd., New Delhi.

Sinha, Shantha, *"Child Labour and Education Policy in India"*, 'The Administrator'—1996, New Age International (Pvt.) Ltd., New Delhi.

Sinha, Amarjeet, *"Educational and Public Action"*, 'The Administrator'—1996, New Age International (Pvt.) Ltd. New Delhi.

Seth, Leila, "Towards a Better Tomorrow", Souvenir, ILI, 1994.

Sinha, Ajoy, "Child Labour related Statistical Profile", 1996 (July-Sept.) 41 Adm. 159-219.

Sinha, Roopashri, *"Violation of Child Rights"*, Economic and Political Weekly, October 8, 1994.

Shastri, Satish, *"Population policy and Law—An Indian Perspective"* Souvenir, ILI 1994.

Sekar, R. Helen, *"Towards better Enforcement of Child Labour Law"*, Fellow, V.V. Giri National Labour Institute, Noida.

Sangal, P.S., *"Agenda 21 Population and Role of Law"* Indian Experience, Souvenir, ILI, 1994.

Subba, Rao, T.V., "Rights to Food Perspective in Law", Souvenir, ILI, 1994.

Sharma, K.S., "Inadequacies in Legislation and Child-care, in India", New Age International (Pvt.) Ltd., New Delhi.

Sinha, K. Rajeev, "Movement Against Child Labour, Policy, Action and Challenges" : An appraisal 1994, 1995, 1996, 9, 10, 11, Kan, L.J. 62-7.

Sankaran, M.V., "Indian Nuclear Power Programme *vis-à-vis* Environmental and Human health", Souvenir, ILI, 1994.

Saxena, Harisharma, *"Bio-Technology Transfer from Developing Countries Scale and Type of Equipment Knowledge and Expertise Among Nations—Environments and Health Issues"*, Souvenir, ILI, 1994.

Tiwari, Y.K., "Deficient Pesticides Law and Protection of Farm Labour", Souvenir, ILI, 1994.

Vilanilam, "World Development and Environment—Towards a More Child-friendly Economic Order in 21st Century", Souvenir, ILI, 1994.

Williams, Christoper, "Environmental Causes of Developmental Disability—A Victim Prospective, Souvenir, ILI, 1994.

Video Review

Kumar, Girish, *"Primary Education In India"*, A Journey, The Administrator, New Age International (Pvt.) Ltd., New Delhi.

Pushpendra and Ajoy Sinha, *"Prayas"* "The Administrator", 1996, New Age International (Pvt.) Ltd., New Delhi.

Puspendra and Ajoy Sinha, *"Whose Children"*, "The Administrator, 1996, New Age International (Pvt.) Ltd., New Delhi.

Puspendra and Ajoy Sinha, *"Withering Buds"*, "The Administrator, 1996, New Age International (Pvt.) Ltd., New Delhi.

The News Papers and Misc.

"The Statesman", 3rd February, 2004.

"The Statesman", 12th February, 2004.

"The Statesman", 16th February, 2004.

"The Statesman" 18th February, 2004.

"The Statesman", 30th April, 2004.

"The Statesman", 26th February, 2005.

"IIPA News Letter", Feb., 2004.

"Employment News", 1-7 May, 2004.

"Booklet under the Services 'Know Your Rights' by NHRC", 2008.

Index